5-84
STRAND PRICE
$ 11 50

D0083380

MODERN GREEK POETRY
Voice and Myth

Edmund Keeley

MODERN GREEK POETRY

Voice and Myth

PRINCETON UNIVERSITY PRESS
PRINCETON, NEW JERSEY

Copyright © 1983 by Princeton University Press

Published by Princeton University Press, 41 William Street, Princeton,
New Jersey 08540
In the United Kingdom: Princeton University Press,
Guildford, Surrey

All Rights Reserved

Library of Congress Cataloging in Publication Data will be found
on the last printed page of this book

ISBN 0-691-06586-1

Publication of this book has been aided by the Whitney Darrow
Publication Reserve Fund of Princeton University Press

This book has been composed in Linotron Sabon

Clothbound editions of Princeton University Press books are printed on
acid-free paper, and binding materials are chosen for
strength and durability

Printed in the United States of America by Princeton University Press
Princeton, New Jersey

Designed by Laury A. Egan

pb

For Kay and Nikos Paleologos
"... these carved reliefs of a humble art."

PA
5250
K44
1983
c1

UWEC McIntrye Library
DISCARDED
EAU CLAIRE, WI

DISCARDED

Contents

ABBREVIATIONS

PREFACE

The essays collected here were written over a period of seventeen years. Two appear here for the first time (or simultaneously in periodicals), and three have been measurably expanded for this collection.[1] More than half can be called recent—1978 to the present—and each of the essays has been supplemented and updated by notes that provide cross-references to the consideration of related issues in other essays. Yet I do not want to pretend to more currency and coherence than the volume actually reveals; I would like to think there is sufficient coherence in my having explored, throughout the collection, those related aspects of form and content implied by the title and outlined more fully below. I have made no attempt to change the earlier essays in style or substance so as to make them conform to what I might take to be a more current critical position or mode. It seemed to me that the dangers of revising and updating in that way were at least equal to the possible benefits. Revisionist procedures and afterthoughts, especially long-delayed ones, are not much more immune from distortion than initial approaches inspired by ardor and reasonably weighed first thoughts, particularly in a world of rapidly shifting critical fashion (my own rela-

[1] "Voice, Perspective, and Context in Cavafy" and "Elytis and the Greek Tradition" are new. "Seferis and the 'Mythical Method,'" "Seferis's 'Political' Voice," and "Ritsos: Voice and Vision in the Shorter Poems" have been substantially expanded. First serial publication of these essays (in abridged form) and the other essays included in this collection is indicated in the "Bibliographical Note."

tively unchanging and therefore rather old-fashioned predispositions as a critic are indicated in the opening essay on Cavafy). I have therefore left the earlier essays as I first wrote them, with only a few substitutions—for example, a "usually" for an "always"—to temper the occasional exaggeration that perhaps resulted from the passion of discovery and an excess of enthusiasm for some emerging point of view. I have also made sure that each essay is addressed, where appropriate, to an English-speaking audience, because that is the audience which this collection is intended to serve first of all, there being so little criticism of contemporary Greek poetry in book form to which English-speaking readers may currently have access.[2]

What struck me on reviewing both early and more recent essays for inclusion here was the growing evidence of constancy I encountered, not simply in my own more or less consistent perspective regarding poets I have been studying and translating since 1950 (that, after all, could be merely the product of stubbornness or obsessiveness), but in the consistently shared preoccupations and aspirations of the poets themselves as these were revealed to me over the years. Without meaning to impose an arbitrary unity on essays written at different times for various occasions, I think it may be helpful, in providing the reader with a just orientation to this

[2] The broadest study of twentieth-century Greek poets in English is still Philip Sherrard's *The Marble Threshing Floor: Studies in Modern Greek Poetry*, originally published by Vallentine, Mitchell, and Co., London, in 1956 and reprinted in 1980 by Denise Harvey and Co., Athens. Sherrard's volume includes helpful essays on Palamas, Cavafy, Sikelianos, and Seferis. George Seferis's *On the Greek Style: Selected Essays in Poetry and Hellenism*, trans. Rex Warner and Th. D. Frangopoulos (New York and London, 1966; reprinted by Denise Harvey, 1982) contains essays on Sikelianos and Cavafy in addition to commentary on Seferis's own work. *Modern Greek Writers*, ed. Edmund Keeley and Peter Bien (Princeton, 1972) includes essays on Palamas, Cavafy, Seferis, and Elytis, but is now out of print. Zissimos Lorenzatos's *The Lost Center and Other Essays in Greek Poetry*, trans. Kay Cicellis (Princeton, 1980) includes an essay on Seferis.

volume, for me to consider here both the persistent terms of my approach to the Greek poets included in this collection and certain of their shared preoccupations that I explore in these essays, in particular those that seem to define important aspects of what might be called the contemporary Greek poetic sensibility.

I take the terms "voice" and "myth" from my title for useful starting points. In directing the reader toward the two principal avenues of my concern, they have the advantage—and disadvantage—of flexibility, the first because it has not yet gained sufficient currency to be bound by a single definition or even a debate over definitions,[3] the second because it has had so much currency for so long that it brings with it a broad range of possibilities. In these essays I have used "voice" to cover a poet's preoccupation with formal matters such as tone, stance, and attitude (as in Cavafy) or style and dramatic modes (as in Sikelianos, Seferis, Elytis, and Ritsos). I have also used it to help designate a poet's perspective or even vision beyond formal representations of voice in individual poems (as in the Cavafy essay and in the essays on Sikelianos's "sublime" voice, Seferis's "political" voice, and the voice of Ritsos's later poems). I have tried to make the relevance of the term and its particular meaning clear within each of the several contexts in which its use seemed to me appropriate and valuable.

Along with these uses of the term for critical exploration, I find that it also serves to identify what the poets themselves have apparently regarded as one of the abiding concerns of every writer in modern Greece: establishing a personal mode of expression within a tradition that goes back almost three thousand years and that brings with it not only a heavy burden of voices out of the past but a language both naturally and arbitrarily in flux and one that is now spoken by only a few million people. It is a concern that Elytis manifests in his Nobel

[3] For example, there was no entry for "voice" in the 1965 edition of the *Encyclopedia of Poetry and Poetics*, ed. Alex Preminger (Princeton); an entry appears for the first time in the 1974 "enlarged edition."

Prize acceptance speech,[4] where he refers to "the difficulties that a poet must face when he attempts to express the things he loves most in words that were once used by Sappho and Pindar, but that are now deprived of the audience, the vast repercussion they had in what was then the entire civilized world," and where he goes on to speak of "the crushing burden" that the Greek language has to bear, one that "you can sense . . . clearly in the poetry of modern Greece." And it is a concern that Seferis identifies as both a personal and a general problem in the conversation that appears as a "Postscript" to these essays. He talks there about the process of refusal that Cavafy had to go through before "he found at last his own personal voice" and thereby came to "*see*." And at another point, with reference to Makriyannis and Seferis's designation of style as "the difficulty encountered when a man tries to express himself,"[5] he tells us something about the difficulty he encountered in establishing his own style, a difficulty compounded both for him and other Greek poets, it would seem, by the "calamity of academic intervention" that complicated the attempt by writers in Greece to create a natural vernacular language, a true modern Greek voice, if you will.

One of the central purposes of these essays has been to illustrate how the best of the contemporary Greek poets succeeded in solving the problem of expressing themselves in the particular language and literary tradition they inherited. As I suggest in the essay on Ritsos, each of the poets discussed in this volume not only created a personal voice but each was able at some crucial point in his career to temper rhetorical self-indulgence or subjective lyricism through the dramatic and symbolic expression of a tragic sense of life. This shared sense, embodied in a mature—if sometimes delayed—vision of the human predicament, often seems to have emerged from

[4] Translated into English for the occasion of the Nobel Prize ceremony by Kay Cicellis (I quote from her typescript).

[5] *On the Greek Style*, p. 61. For a list of short titles used in this volume, see the "Bibliographical Note."

a catharsis that was more than merely stylistic, but in each case it found its most effective expression in poetry of relative simplicity, economy, and objectivity.

The second of my persistent terms, "myth," offers another access to the general problem of how a contemporary Greek poet is to succeed in accommodating his rich—sometimes too rich—past while developing a personal voice and mode. In this context the problem is related to what has frequently been called the Greek writer's search for his national identity, or what Elytis describes as the attempt by the poets of his time "to find the true face of Greece." This attempt has consistently confronted the issues of what is truly a native resource and what a foreign import (e.g., Byzantium versus the European Renaissance), of what deserves the name of Hellenism and what doesn't, and where the poet is to look for the most vital sources in the long Greek tradition. Each of the poets considered in these essays conducted his search for the true face of Greece in his own way and arrived at his own resolution, and in the case of each, myth in some form was a major vehicle in bringing the search to a productive end. Cavafy created his own Alexandrian myth to embody his personal vision, supported by a complex image of diaspora Hellenism. Sikelianos drew on a variety of ancient sources in shaping a personal mythology that could accommodate pre-classical, classical, and Christian elements and that could transmit, with increasing effectiveness as his career progressed, the vital connections between the natural and the supernatural, the physical and the metaphysical, worlds. Seferis created an enduring image of "contemporary sorrow" and "thirsting despair" by manipulating his particular parallel between the mythology of Homer and Aeschylus and the contemporary experience of travelers in an arid Greek landscape and seascape searching for—among other things—the "other life" of a vanished past. Elytis, worried about the excessive influence of Renaissance neoclassicism, began his attempt to accommodate the past by exploiting what he called the ancient "mechanism of myth-making ... without evoking any mythical figures" and by drawing more and more on resources in the Byzantine and modern Greek demotic traditions; but in some of his best work, he reveals a subtle manipulation of ancient myth to shape an image of the contemporary Greek sensibility in keeping with the practice of Sikelianos and Seferis. Ritsos both creates his own mythical stories by presenting ancient characters in modern dress (usually in longer dramatic forms) and, in his shorter poems, also uses allusions to the ancient Greek and Christian traditions in order to illustrate the mutilation and sometimes the transformation of past gods and heroes by the violent dislocations of contemporary history.

Some of the essays that follow focus specifically on a given poet's use of myth in shaping his mature voice and vision, but there is no essay in which the poet's relation to his nation's past is not a central concern in some form, and that in itself illustrates the constancy of this preoccupation. That each of these five poets was not only able to find a just resolution of the problem of accommodating the Greek past that he inherited but was also able in the end to turn it to his advantage in creating a personal voice that speaks in some measure both to the national experience and to the larger human predicament may explain why these particular poets, along with Palamas, have now emerged as the most important representatives in this century of a revitalized tradition in poetry that is the longest continuing tradition in the Western world. It is surely one reason why they are worthy of broader attention.

I want to thank Denise Harvey for helpful suggestions regarding the organization and expansion of these essays and Peter Bien and George Savidis for their generous reading of the full text. I also want to thank the National Endowment for the Arts, the Rockefeller Foundation Study Center at Bellagio, and the Princeton University Committees on Hellenic Studies and on Research in the Humanities and Social Sciences for grants in support of my work on this volume.

Princeton, New Jersey
Spring, 1982

MODERN GREEK POETRY
Voice and Myth

Voice, Perspective, and Context in Cavafy

Criticism of poetry in Greece has been mostly spared both the virtues and vices promoted by the New Criticism in English-speaking countries. The principal virtues—those of a better understanding and a larger appreciation of individual poems through a close reading of the text—are rarely in evidence. At the same time, the failure of the New Criticism to give appropriate weight to context—historical, literary, linguistic, biographical—is generally not a defect of Greek criticism. One might argue that too much weight is still given to matters of literary history and literary definition and too little to what must remain the primary function of criticism when it is performed generously: aiding readers to understand and relish the best work of the best poets. Cavafy serves as a case in point. And two recent articles by unusually sophisticated critics of Cavafy, Nasos Vayenas and Roderick Beaton, provide an occasion for reviewing both new and familiar critical approaches to the most important and subtle of Greek poets in this century.

Vayenas's piece[1] outlines the attempt of a number of Greek critics to solve what Vayenas calls "the problem" of Cavafy. A major aspect of the problem is seen to be that of finding

[1] "The Language of Irony (Towards a Definition of the Poetry of Cavafy)," *Byzantine and Modern Greek Studies*, Vol. 5 (1979), pp. 43-56. Portions of his essay first appeared in Greek in *The Poet and the Dancer: An Examination of the Poetics and Poetry of Seferis* (Athens, 1979), Chapter 1, section 4 (see especially pp. 95-102).

an appropriate definition—really a categorization—of Cava-
fy's work, preferably in a single word. Dimaras, the great
literary historian of modern Greece, suggested "lyric." Seferis
challenged this, at least for a time, with the term "didactic,"
then preferred "dramatic." Vayenas makes his case for the
term "ironic." Of course no single term is sufficient in itself
to describe Cavafy's work over the course of his career. All
four terms are to some degree relevant, depending on the
period of Cavafy's work in question and the character of
individual poems, and sometimes all four might be brought
to bear on a single poem. An even less fruitful aspect of "the
problem" is posed by the questions " 'How could [Cavafy]
write poetry when his expressive means were those of prose?' "
and " 'How could poetry transmit emotion when its language
was not emotive, that is, not poetic?' "[2] Vayenas traces the
suggested "solutions" offered by Agras, Nikolareizis, Dallas,
and Seferis, but finds each too limited to resolve the mystery
of Cavafy's presumably unpoetic poetic. Vayenas concludes
that "the problem of his poetry is not beyond solution"[3] if
one looks at his use of irony.

For those interested in exploring the poems themselves with
new insight and recognition, these questions seem remote, and
the so-called problem remains in the realm of theoretical rather
than practical criticism. W. H. Auden provided the key to a
different approach in his introduction to the Rae Dalven trans-
lation of Cavafy,[4] where he offered the phrase "tone of voice"
to characterize what was "unique" about Cavafy and where
he implicitly indicated the futility of a debate over definitions
of the kind presented in Vayenas's article. Auden states that
"a unique tone of voice cannot be described; it can only be
imitated, that is to say, either parodied or quoted."[5] And with
this remark he leads the reader back to the poetry itself, which
is its own definition, requiring no all-encompassing charac-

[2] Ibid., p. 43.
[3] Ibid., p. 51.
[4] *The Complete Poems of Cavafy* (New York, 1976), pp. vii-xv. The essay
also appears in *Forewords and Afterwords* (New York, 1973).
[5] Ibid., p. ix.

terization of categorization for those who will give the poems a sensitive reading. Fortunately Vayenas does not limit himself to the theoretical "problem" he explores but uses his "solution" to provide new insight into several of Cavafy's more complicated—and often misunderstood—poems, as we shall see below.

Auden's term "tone of voice" is a more helpful guide to the work (even if he himself points to its inadequacy) than any definition he might have attempted, and so is his elaboration of its implications: "Reading any poem of [Cavafy's] I feel: 'This reveals a person with a unique perspective on the world' "[6] Voice and perspective are the terms that give us access to a better understanding of Cavafy's subtleties. Auden's remarks imply that there is a tone of voice in Cavafy's poetry, a "personal speech,"[7] that colors the speaking voice in any particular poem, as there is a "perspective on the world" that colors the attitude in any particular poem. The tone of voice and the perspective are strong enough, in Auden's view, to emerge through any translation: "I have read translations of Cavafy made by many different hands, but every one of them was immediately recognizable as a poem by Cavafy; nobody else could possibly have written it."[8]

Tone of voice, in this view, is obviously more than a matter of personal style and particular language, since these are mostly lost in translation (one is compelled to add here that Cavafy's language is special enough to contribute significantly to his tone of voice in Greek, however one interprets the phrase). As I understand Auden's remarks, what he has in mind is the poet's particular way of presenting his material and the perspective that emerges from this presentation, and I agree that these add up to a unique "voice" that not only colors individual poems but that implies a certain unified sensibility in his work. Still, Cavafy's presentation is varied and often complex, and arriving at the perspective that colors individual poems is not as easy or immediate as Auden's remarks may

[6] Ibid., p. viii.
[7] Ibid.
[8] Ibid.

5

suggest. It is often an exercise that requires unusual tact and a heightened sensitivity to the poetry's context. Evidence of the difficulty is the considerable disagreement even among Cavafy's best critics about the perspective that emerges in specific instances and some disagreement about whether there is what can be called a perspective at all.

In developing his mature voice, Cavafy went through a period of experimentation with various modes—lyric, didactic, narrative, and dramatic among them[9]—and these modes continued to play their role in shaping the poetry of his mature period; but if we focus on his work from 1910 forward, I think we will find general agreement among his recent critics that the starting point in gaining access to his poems is a consideration of the poet's stance in a given poem—what an older generation of critics might have called the particular mask the poet chose to wear in specific instances. Even if the poet's "unique tone of voice" generally colors his work, there is still inevitably some stance in Cavafy, whether the poet chooses to speak in the first person, or act as narrator, or address a character in the second person, or take on the role of a character in a dramatic monologue. It is in Cavafy's narrations and dramatic monologues that the poet's voice— that is, the voice behind the mask—is the most muted, often heard by way of irony alone (as Vayenas suggests), often discernible only by a careful examination of the poem's tone and context (I use the term "tone" here in the standard sense of the speaker's attitude in the poem, sometimes quite at odds with the poet's attitude and usually distinguished from it by at least the distance that the term "persona" is meant to suggest).

The difficulty of determining the character of Cavafy's stance in the first instance, and of his voice and perspective in the second, in some of his more subtle (and usually late) poems is illustrated by the divergent interpretations of the two dramatic monologues that Vayenas discusses at the conclusion

[9] See Edmund Keeley, *Cavafy's Alexandria: Study of a Myth in Progress* (Cambridge and London, 1976), Chapter 2.

of his essay, "On the Outskirts of Antioch" (1932/33) and "A Great Procession of Priests and Laymen" (1926). Both of these belong to the cycle of poems having to do with Julian the Apostate, a cycle that includes six poems in the "canon," one so-called "unpublished poem," and five more previously unpublished poems that surfaced recently.[10]

The Julian poems constitute by far the largest group devoted to the same historical character in Cavafy's work. It is therefore exceedingly difficult to consider any single poem in the cycle outside the context of others in the group; in fact, I would suggest that the critic who does so, and who also doesn't consider this group in its relation to Cavafy's late mode and voice in general, proceeds perilously. In any case, the starting point is correctly perceived by Vayenas to be that of determining the stance and tone of the poems. The speaking voice in both poems—the poet's mask, if you will—is that of a Christian who represents the Christians of Antioch during

[10] The term "unpublished poem" has become the standard one in designating those poems that Cavafy did not himself publish during his lifetime and that first appeared in G. P. Savidis's edition Ἀνέκδοτα Ποιήματα (Unpublished poems). "Julian at the Mysteries" is so designated, and though "On the Outskirts of Antioch" was published for the first time after Cavafy's death, it appeared in the 1935 posthumous volume, published in Alexandria, that established the so-called canon. The five additional "unpublished poems" appeared for the first time, judiciously edited by Renata Lavagnini, in "The Unpublished Drafts of Five Poems on Julian the Apostate," *Byzantine and Modern Greek Studies*, Vol. 7 (1981), pp. 55-88. In the same issue (pp. 89-104), G. W. Bowersock offers a perceptive and authoritative commentary on the five poems and on the group as a whole in his "The Julian Poems of C. P. Cavafy." He shows, among other significant things, how keen Cavafy was to be historically accurate. He also demonstrates that in the Julian poems Cavafy "concerned himself with a rather small number of topics from the range of those that were possible . . . Julian's childhood, Julian at Antioch, and Julian's death," and that the "common denominator for every single one of the poems—what links the principal motifs together—is Christianity" (p. 101). Bowersock sees the poems confirming how important Antioch was as a symbol in Cavafy of both permissive Christianity and appropriate Hellenism or Greekness. He concludes: "In the Julian poems he struggled for historical accuracy because it was clearly imperative for him to know that there really had been a world that could accommodate a sensualist, both Christian and Greek" (pp. 103-104).

Julian's short reign, A.D. 361-363, in the one instance shortly before the end of that reign, and in the other shortly after. Seferis's reading of the two poems implicitly assumes an identity between the poet and his speaker, thus promoting an interpretation that sees the poems as an expression of Cavafy's total sympathy with the Christians of Antioch and their ridicule of Julian's pagan pretensions. Vayenas shrewdly challenges this view of Cavafy's attitude by pointing out that the tone of both poems—that is, the speaker's attitude in each—indicates a "magnitude of . . . hatred for Julian" inconsistent with the indications of Christian piety in the poems, and this contradiction serves to suggest the "magnitude of the Christians' hypocrisy," a hypocrisy that is seen to have its origins in the Antiochians' "strong distaste for Julian's ascetic version of the ancient worship, the application of which would result in a code of behaviour not unlike that prescribed by Christianity."[11] Vayenas therefore regards Seferis's assumption in the case of "On the Outskirts of Antioch," that the poem "is simply an attack against Julian and that Cavafy is on the side of Babylas and the Christians and against the ancients," as a misinterpretation. And in the case of "A Great Procession of Priests and Laymen," he challenges Seferis's view that the poem is "an unfavourable comment on Julian" and Seferis's opinion that the last line of the poem should be declaimed "in the reverent tone appropriate to the prayers of the divine liturgy." In Vayenas's opinion, the line should be used in an ironic tone of voice "to call into question the genuineness of the emotion so skillfully created in the preceding lines."[12]

There is some merit in this reconsideration of Seferis's position, but it is not a full enough account of either poem's implications nor a sufficient designation of Cavafy's perspective. Let us review the poems in turn. The speaker in "On the Outskirts of Antioch" is depicted as being not so much hypocritical as arrogant in his defense of his martyr Babylas (or

[11] "The Language of Irony," p. 54.
[12] Ibid., p. 55.

8

Vavylas);[13] his attitude toward Julian is too close to what he portrays Julian's to be in dismissing the martyr. The speaker shows us Julian losing his temper and shouting: ". . . take him away immediately, this Vavylas. / You there, do you hear? He gets on Apollo's nerves. / Grab him, raise him at once, / dig him out, take him wherever you want, / take him away, throw him out. This isn't a joke. . . ." Whether or not the speaker's rendering of Julian's tone is accurate, the speaker's own tone gives him away for being similarly arrogant and intolerant— if more subtle in his manner of expression—as he brings his irony to bear in revealing the destruction he and his fellow Christians have wrought in taking their revenge on Julian:

> And hasn't the temple done brilliantly since!
> In no time at all a colossal fire broke out,
> a terrible fire,
> and both the temple and Apollo burned to the ground.
> Ashes the idol: dirt to be swept away.

> Julian blew up, and he spread it around—
> What else could he do?—that we, the Christians,
> had set the fire. Let him say so.
> It hasn't been proved. Let him say so.
> The essential thing is: he blew up.

The essential thing is that this Christian speaker has cast out Julian's pagan god—in spirit if not in fact—as mercilessly and fanatically as he depicts Julian's treatment of Vavylas. An eye for an eye; no charity here. And the speaker reveals a rather amusing hangover of paganism in himself when he gives the pagan gods more life and reality than one might think a pious Christian has any business giving them (though the hangover

---

[13] In the Keeley-Sherrard version, *C. P. Cavafy: Collected Poems,* ed. George Savidis (Princeton and London, 1975), pp. 383 and 385. Unless otherwise designated, subsequent quotations from Cavafy's work in English are from this volume.

is of course historically accurate):[14] "It was [Vavylas] the false god hinted at, him he feared. / As long as he felt him near he didn't dare / pronounce his oracle: not a murmur. / (The false gods are terrified of our martyrs.)"

If the speaker condemns himself by showing the same arrogant intolerance of Julian that he has Julian demonstrate toward "this Vavylas," can the reader trust the image of Julian that the speaker projects? The answer to this seems to me to reside in the poem's context, both the historical context that it presupposes and whatever relevant knowledge of the poet's mature voice we can bring to the poem. We know from history that Julian did indeed order the church that the Christians built over Vavylas's tomb to be demolished and the relic of Vavylas to be removed, and we also know that he was intolerant of those who professed to teach while "harbor[ing] in their souls opinions irreconcilable with the spirit of the state," namely the spirit of Emperor Julian's austere paganism.[15] Whether or not the speaker catches the exact tone of Julian's intolerance, he has the substance of it right. And other of Cavafy's Julian poems would seem to provide the kind of gloss on this one that suggests the poet is sympathetic toward the speaker's image of the emperor.

Two earlier poems are particularly relevant in this connection, "Julian Seeing Contempt" (1923) and "Julian and the Antiochians" (1926). Neither is a dramatic monologue; in

[14] As G. W. Bowersock puts it ("The Julian Poems," p. 101), "the Christians of Julian's time were, after all, for the most part yesterday's pagans. They had not changed their way of life all that much. At Antioch they went to the theater and the chariot races, and they celebrated their festivals as they had before. When Julian entered the city he heard the ill-omened wailing of the festival of Adonis. Cavafy understood all this rather better than most historians. . . ."

[15] A. A. Vasiliev, *History of the Byzantine Empire*, Vol. 1 (Madison, 1968), p. 73. And Bowersock tells us ("The Julian Poems," p. 101) that the characteristics of Julian which Cavafy chose to underscore were hypocrisy and puritanical intolerance, and he adds: "The sources provide ample justification for characterizing the emperor in this way, even if many writers have preferred different assessments. Julian was an ascetic who demanded strict adherence to the principles of his new pagan church."

both the poet enters the poem through a persona who com-
ments on the historical moment that the poem dramatizes, as
close as Cavafy comes to making a direct statement in his
mature work. In the first, the persona mocks Julian for at-
tempting to incite and goad his "friends," among whom Julian
finds great contempt for the gods, friends who "weren't Chris-
tians" but who also weren't ready to go so far as to "play"—
as Julian ironically could, having been brought up a Chris-
tian—with a new religious system that the persona calls "lu-
dicrous in theory and application." Julian's friends were Greeks,
after all, guided still—the persona implies—by the ancient
maxim "Nothing in excess." This image of Julian as a man
given at times to ludicrous excess is not out of keeping with
the Julian who loses his temper in casting out the martyr
Vavylas. Nor is the image of Julian that we find in "Julian
and the Antiochians," where the persona contrasts Julian's
"hot air about the false gods, / his boring self-advertisement,
/ his childish fear of the theater, / his graceless prudery, his
ridiculous beard" with the notorious, immoral, quite un-
Christian but nevertheless "beautiful" and "delectable" way
of life of Christian Antiochians, which "consummated a union
between Art / and the erotic proclivities of the flesh" and
which was always in "absolute good taste." The persona asks
rhetorically whether it could ever have been possible for the
Antiochians to give up the latter out of an allegiance to the
former. He concludes that of course they preferred the more
tolerant, less puritanical regime of Apostate Julian's Christian
predecessors.

The theme of excess and the intolerance it engenders is what
links these two poems to the later "On the Outskirts of An-
tioch" and what helps to clarify the poet's perspective in the
later poem. Both the Christian speaker in the poem and "un-
holy" Julian demonstrate a like propensity for excess; both
are given to fanaticism and intolerance toward those with
opposing beliefs. Cavafy's perspective emerges from the in-
terplay between the juxtaposed representations of excess in
the poem. In this instance he sides with neither the Christian
speaker nor the pagan emperor; his perspective, most aptly

characterized by the maxim "Nothing in excess," transcends both.[16] And that is generally the case. Even in the poem "Julian and the Antiochians," where the persona's irony—really sarcasm—is mostly at Julian's expense, we have that passing note on the Christians' excess: "Immoral to a degree—and probably more than a degree—they certainly were . . ."—an ominous note if one is aware of the close relation between the Christian way of life depicted in this poem and that of Cavafy's ancient Alexandrians, especially those commemorated in several of the "epitaphs" he wrote between 1914 and 1918, where the union between elegance, beauty, youth, art, and the erotic proclivities of the flesh is shown to have its dark side; "I, Iasis, lie here—famous for my good looks / in this great city . . . / excess wore me out, killed me. Traveler, / if you're an Alexandrian, you won't blame me. / You know the pace of our life—its fever, its absolute devotion to pleasure" (from "Tomb of Iasis").

Joseph Brodsky tells us in his generally illuminating essay-review on Cavafy[17] that the poet "did not choose between paganism and Christianity but was swinging between them like a pendulum." One might modify the metaphor by suggesting that it is the speaking voice that does the swinging; Cavafy's perspective is what holds the pendulum in place, aloof from the action, not taking sides except when arrogance, fanaticism, intolerance, hubris, or other excess earns his irony. Brodsky points out that Cavafy's "most vigorous ironies were directed against one of the main vices of Christianity—pious intolerance." We have seen that Julian is also shown to have had his moments of pious intolerance, but in "A Great Proces-

---

[16] This conclusion not only challenges Vayenas's view of Cavafy's perspective in both poems but also my own in *Cavafy's Alexandria* (p. 121), where I fail to make a proper distinction between the implications of the tone in the dramatic monologues about Julian and those Julian poems in which Cavafy speaks through a persona. I say, erroneously, that "the tone of each [monologue] makes it clear that the poet sides with the Christian speaker."

[17] *The New York Review of Books*, Feb. 17, 1977, pp. 32-34.

sion of Priests and Laymen," it is the Christian vice that sets the poem's tone, as Vayenas suggests in challenging Seferis's reading of the poem (though he does not indicate exactly what it is in the text that promotes his own "ironic" reading). The speaker here is kin to the Christian speaker in "On the Outskirts of Antioch." He may not express himself with the same degree of sarcasm, but he is equally intolerant in his view of Julian, calling him "unholy" (μιαρότατος) and "appalling" (ἀποτρόπαιος). More to the point, he mocks Julian's pagan followers, "lately so full of arrogance," for slinking away from the Christian procession, and sees it as good riddance "as long as they don't renounce their errors." In the Cavafian context, this kind of language and this point of view clearly set the stage for a fall from grace. "Pious" self-satisfaction and arrogant disdain carry in them the seeds of their own destruction; if the "arrogant" pagans have had their day, one can expect that the infallible ("as long as they don't renounce their errors") and self-satisfied Christians will have theirs too.

It is this typically Cavafian perspective—which, incidentally, Seferis was the first to identify, at least implicitly, in his commentary on "Alexander Jannaios and Alexandra"—[18] that most compels an ironic reading of the poem's concluding line. And the irony is not only a matter of tone (the hypocrisy behind the Christians' "piety" that Vayenas sees as the determinant of the line's tone—in his use of the term really the poet's rather than the speaker's attitude—is not as clearly represented in this poem as it is in "On the Outskirts of Antioch," though it is part of the Cavafian context that one can legitimately bring to the poem). The dominant irony at the end of the poem is what we traditionally call dramatic irony. The speaker sees "the empire delivered at last" because "appalling Julian" has been replaced by "most pious Jovian," who is now to be the object of Christian prayers. What the speaker does not know—while the reader presumably does—

[18] *On the Greek Style*, pp. 147-149. See also *Cavafy's Alexandria*, p. 185, n. 10.

is that pious, tolerant, and relatively ineffectual Jovian will reign for only seven months (until February, A.D. 364), Christianity will triumph but will also be marked by constant strife and contention, the empire will soon divide permanently under Valentinian in the West and Valens in the East, and within less than a century, the Western empire will have fallen irretrievably. The irony is underlined in Cavafian terms by a passage in Gibbon, one of Cavafy's principal historical sources, as he meditates on the death of Valentinian the Third in A.D. 455 and the doom of Rome: ". . . even his religion was questionable; and though he never deviated into the paths of heresy, he scandalized the pious Christians by his attachment to the profane arts of magic and divination. . . . The severe inquisition, which confiscated their goods and tortured their persons, compelled the subjects of Valentinian to prefer the more simple tyranny of the Barbarians. . . . If all the Barbarian conquerors had been annihilated in the same hour, their total destruction would not have restored the empire of the West; and, if Rome still survived, she survived the loss of freedom, of virtue, and of honour."[19]

The historical context of which the speaker is unaware, source of the poem's dramatic irony, is what Seferis would call the missing statue on Cavafy's pedestal.[20] As in several of Cavafy's subtlest late poems—"Alexander Jannaios and Alexandra" and "In the Year 200 B.C." in particular—it is events that follow on the speaker's heels which provide the poem's final comment, outside the range of the speaker's voice and perception, the kind of silent comment that (as I have suggested elsewhere)[21] raises the poet's perspective above the speaker's particular bias to the level of the poet-historian who sees a more universal—and generally tragic—pattern behind even those moments of history with which he has shown some degree of sympathetic identification (as was manifest in this instance in "Julian and the Antiochians"). The poet's per-

[19] Ed. Bury, Vol. III (London, 1908), pp. 479-480.

[20] See n. 18 above.

[21] *Cavafy's Alexandria*, pp. 147-148. I attempt to offer a detailed account of Cavafy's perspective in this study, especially in Chapters Five and Six.

spective may be seen as a usually unspoken conscience that recognizes any individual success and any specific historical change as subject to reversal by the gods, that sometimes serves to warn against those excesses that lead to fanaticism, intolerance, or self-satisfied complacency, and that sometimes finds wisdom and courage to reside in a recognition of human limitations.

It is this perspective that seems to me to be a fundamental aspect of Cavafy's mature voice, an aspect of the "unique perspective on the world" that Auden saw stamped on every Cavafy poem, even in translation. One might find other terms in which to express the perspective as it relates to individual poems, and one might find its presence more or less overt, but an awareness of its role is often valuable—and sometimes essential—in establishing the force and meaning of Cavafy's more complex poems. It is not enough, in my opinion, to see Cavafy as simply an ironist, though he surely is that at times. And in any case, one has to be sensitive to the context, the pattern of thought and sensibility, within which his irony operates if one is to understand its full implications.

Roderick Beaton, in his provocative article "C. P. Cavafy: Irony and Hellenism,"[22] appears to be somewhat out of sympathy with this position. Following the lead given by Vayenas, Beaton argues, persuasively at times, that Cavafy was "a fully conscious ironist" and that the emotional impact of his poems derives "not from sensuousness of the language, nor from the intensity of a 'vision' . . . but from the vivid juxtaposition of contradictory emotions, of things seen from contradictory angles, of contradictory 'visions.' "[23] This is not a "structuralist" position (though that school of criticism is invoked at one point)[24] which might find meanings in the text—literal, ironic, otherwise—that the poet did not necessarily intend but that are there to be discovered nevertheless in the structure of the text; Beaton is concerned with identifying ironies and contra-

[22] *The Slavonic and East European Review*, Vol. 59, No. 4 (1981), pp. 516-528.
[23] Ibid., p. 518.
[24] Ibid., p. 523, n. 18.

dictory "visions" that Cavafy fully intended, as a "fully conscious ironist" would presumably have to have. He goes on to tell us that irony "is all-pervasive in Cavafy's poetry and nothing in his poetic world is sacred. . . ." He finds that Cavafy created "a world of shifting relativities" and that he used irony "not to debunk certain attitudes and characters, nor in support of convictions or a world-view of his own, but in order to create an autonomous dramatic world," one that "in its paradoxes and its relativities, in the richness and at the same time hollowness of its appearances, and in its refusal of any ultimate, profound truth" is a powerful metaphor for "the outside world as it has often been perceived in the twentieth century."[25]

It is hard to take issue with this position without seeming to be rather naive, or insensitive to the poet's complex ironies, or pretentiously in search of profundities, or—to introduce a personal note struck by Beaton—given to "impos[ing] on Cavafy's work a structure and world-view which do not always emerge naturally from [Cavafy's] texts."[26] The term "world-view" is a grand one that I have always found suspiciously vague, but if it implies what Auden calls Cavafy's "perspective on the world," then I would have to admit—in keeping with what I've already indicated—that I do indeed believe there is a perspective in his work; and if the term "structure" implies that there is an interrelation between Cavafy's poems in mode and attitude, and that a pattern of images and attitudes emerges from this interrelation—what I have here called the voice and perspective of his poetry—then I admit to that position as well (though of course I cannot agree that these do not emerge naturally from his texts without proposing a non sequitur). The danger of seeing Cavafy's world as one characterized entirely by shifting relativities in which the poet's irony is never used "to support his own convictions" is that the critic has little solid basis for determining the object of the poet's

[25] Ibid., pp. 527-528. The phrase "a world of shifting relativities" appears on p. 519.

[26] Ibid., p. 517.

irony in specific instances. Without a firm foundation in perspective and context, one begins to see irony everywhere, hear it everywhere, find one's sense of the poet's irony undercut by another irony, and that by the irony of this undercutting. In short, it becomes difficult to establish exactly when the poet intends irony and exactly what he intends to be ironic about.

In actual practice, Beaton's relativist position is qualified by what he himself calls "the context of Cavafy's work," and this leads to some perceptive and helpful criticism of individual poems based on a proper sensitivity to dramatic form, tone, and historical background—as in his subtle reading of "Dangerous Things." But some of his readings seem to me too clever by half, and their identification of levels of irony is occasionally misleading. His interpretation of "Ionic," for example, draws heavily on the context of Cavafy's work for its substantiation but is finally overwhelmed by ironies that do not, in my opinion, emerge naturally from the text of the poem and that in any case serve to diminish its intended impact on the reader. Context is first invoked to "undermine the literal reading" of the poem by emphasizing that the speaking voice, the poem's "we," has "an actual concrete existence in a specific historical period," and "as always in a poem by Cavafy," this suggests a distancing that allows us to view the speaker with some detachment, even irony.[27] Beaton then invokes the context of Cavafy's poetry in terms of mode by pointing to the role of apostrophe in his work and, in this particular poem, the use of a convention that the poet "does not normally use." Finally, he brings to bear two attitudes that are part of the Cavafian perspective—"Cavafy had no time for romanticism" and he "was perversely unaffected by the beauties of nature"—to help the reader determine how he is to read the poem's concluding image.

This use of context raises an impertinent question: if the critic were to say that Cavafy's aptitude for using history to

[27] Quotations from Beaton's commentary on this poem are taken from ibid., pp. 526-527.

achieve an ironic distancing, his occasional manipulation of lyrical excess (as in the case of the apostrophe mentioned here), his anti-romanticism, and his indifference to nature are all part of the structure, the pattern of modes, attitudes, and even convictions, that constitute the poet's mature voice and perspective, would the critic be courting censure for imposing too much structure on Cavafy's autonomous, relativist dramatic world, as Beaton suggests I do in *Cavafy's Alexandria*. Presumably not, because without an awareness of these attitudes and convictions, of the context they create, the critic cannot hope to make his way through Cavafy's world, with its constant possibilities of irony, and find a just reading of individual poems.

My own reading of "Ionic" is not entirely congruent with Beaton's, because the context I bring to the poem promotes less irony and more legitimate lyricism than he discovers, and I find a different emphasis in the poem's tone and syntax. I would agree for a start that to read "Ionic" simply "as a nostalgic evocation of the pagan past of Hellenism and assertion of its essential continuity" may be "quite satisfactory" but is hardly a sufficient account of the poem's subtleties or of its vitality (I take it to be one of the most striking and beautiful of Cavafy's relatively early poems; a first version was published in 1896, the poem was rewritten in 1905 and published again in 1911).[28] Yet, to see a central irony in the poem emerging from the presumed contradiction between "the austere piety which motivated the destruction of the [pagan] temples" and "the slightly naughty ethereal vision of the poem's last three lines" is to restrict and to distort the poem's implications. Let me first offer a version of the full poem:

> That we've broken their statues,
> that we've driven them out of their temples,
> doesn't mean at all that the gods are dead.
> O land of Ionia, they're still in love with you,

[28] See *Cavafy: Collected Poems*, p. 500, note on "Ionic."

their souls still keep your memory.
When an August dawn wakes over you,
your atmosphere is potent with their life,
and sometimes a young ethereal figure,
indistinct, in rapid flight,
wings across your hills.

In arriving at his ironic reading, Beaton indicates an in-
tended contrast between "the speaker's lyricism and manifest
love of beauty in the present" and "his own complicity in the
pious destruction of beauty in the past." Since the speaker
"nowhere refers to a change of heart," he remains "unaware
of the contradiction between the attitudes he expresses," and
"the irony of this poem is that the lyrical nostalgia for pagan
Hellenism is put into the mouth of one of the very people who
helped to destroy it." This presumably "undermines the lyr-
icism of the poem and the speaker's claim to admire beauty
or the Greek past."

This interpretation strikes me as more than too clever by
half. It is true that by using the plural "we" the speaker iden-
tifies himself at the start as a Christian who by implication—
and implication alone—shares in the responsibility for break-
ing the pagan statues and driving the pagan gods from their
temples, but it is not his supposed complicity in "austere piety"
that this identification underlines, presumably in order to es-
tablish a contradiction between this and other "attitudes he
expresses." "Austere piety" is in any case not among the at-
titudes he expresses, nor is it dramatized in the poem. One
could in fact argue that the speaker's use of the strong terms
"σπάσαμε" (broke or broke down) and "διώξαμεν" (threw
out) to describe the Christians' deed actually implies some
distance between his attitude and that of his perhaps austerely
pious but certainly intolerantly destructive fellow Christians.
Neither does the speaker express a "shallow and sentimental"
nostalgia for "the artistic beauty" associated with pagan Hel-
lenism, as Beaton writes, nor does he "claim to admire beauty
or the Greek past"—and since he does not express these var-

ious attitudes, he cannot logically "refer to a change of heart" or be the object of the poet's irony for being unaware of the contradiction between them.

What the speaker does express is his view that, for all the Christians' attempt to get rid of the pagan gods by destroying their statues and driving them out of their temples, the gods are not dead. The implication is that the destruction of statues and temples is not enough to do in the gods because their vision, their ardor—the "σφρῖγος" of their life—[29] is focused and housed elsewhere. With some lyrical fervor the speaker goes on to say "O land of Ionia, you they love still, / you their souls remember still"; that is the emphasis of the Greek syntax: "Ὦ γῆ τῆς Ἰωνίας, *σένα* ἀγαποῦν ἀκόμη, / *σένα* ἡ ψυχές των ἐνθυμοῦνται ἀκόμη" (emphasis mine). In fact, the gods still love and remember Ionia in their souls so ardently that on an August morning one can still feel the youthful exuberance of their life (existence) passing through the air and sometimes actually see the young ethereal figure of a god, indistinct and with hurried pace, crossing above the Ionian hills. The lyricism of the poem does not so much celebrate the speaker's love of beauty or the Greek past as—in keeping with the poem's title—it celebrates the land of Ionia, still home for the souls of the gods who cannot forsake their love of it nor forget what it represents for them.

This celebrative purpose might even excuse the speaker's unusual use of the apostrophe "O land of Ionia." In any case, it is not a "romantic landscape" that Ionia represents but a sensual landscape. When dawn breaks, what appears is not the beauty of nature but a god in the shape of an ephebe (ἐφηβικὴ μορφή). And if there is irony in the poem, it is a rather mild kind, consistent with a typical Cavafian emphasis, and it emerges not from the poet "undermin[ing] the poem's lyricism" or undermining his unaware speaker, but from his

[29] Pring, in *The Oxford Dictionary of Modern Greek* (1965) defines "σφρῖγος" as "youthful exuberance." Kyriakides, in his *Modern Greek-English Dictionary*, published at the time the poem was written (Athens, 1909), offers "vigor; strength, pith, ardor, exuberance."

showing us a Christian who has to acknowledge—even cel-
ebrate the fact—that there is territory presumably beautiful
and sensual enough for the gods to haunt whatever destruction
Christianity may choose to wreak on it, and that, in this
Cavafian context, what is most likely to remain alive to the
bitter end in such territory is a god in the un-Christian shape
of what Beaton translates as "an ethereal boyish form." Also,
if "Morning Sea" is to be seen as a gloss on this poem,[30] it is
not the poet's "subvert[ing] the convention of romantic land-
scape poetry" that is relevant (there is no description of ro-
mantic landscape in "Ionic"—just the mention of dawn break-
ing) but the poet's invoking of those "memories, the images
(idols) of sensual pleasure" which move in to replace the per-
sona's momentary contemplation of sea and shore in "Morn-
ing Sea."

A more revealing gloss on "Ionic" is the poem "Oropher-
nis," where we find a related bit of rhetoric celebrating Ionia
(the poem was written in 1904, a year before "Ionic" was
given its second version):[31]

> Oh those exquisite Ionian nights
> when fearlessly, and entirely in a Greek way,
> he came to know sensual pleasure totally.
> In his heart, Asiatic always,
> but in manners and language, a Greek;
> with his turquoise jewelry, his Greek clothes,
> his body perfumed with oil of jasmine,
> he was the most handsome, the most perfect
> of Ionia's handsome young men.

This pre-Christian image of Orophernis could perhaps serve
as a model for the "ἐφηβικὴ μορφή" (ephebic form) of "Ionic."
In any case, it carries connotations that suggest why—again

---

[30] Beaton, "Cavafy," pp. 526–527. Beaton quotes his own version of "Morning
Sea"; another version can be found in *Cavafy: Collected Poems*, p. 109.

[31] See *Cavafy: Collected Poems*, p. 405, note on "Orophernis." 1904 is
also the year in which Cavafy began to write erotic poetry in the first person.

in the Cavafian context—the gods might indeed still haunt the Ionian landscape after the Christian destruction and why one of Them (shades of "One of Their Gods") might appear on an August morning and pass before a Christian with at least enough of Cavafy's hedonistic bias[32] in him to know one of the reasons pagan Greek Ionia was—and to some degree still is—worthy of celebration.

In his discussion of another poem that presumably lends itself to an ironic reading, "Epitaph of Antiochos, King of Kommagini" (1923), Beaton shrewdly points to the crucial ninth line, the center of the poem, and analyzes its implications with some tact: for a Greek sophist from Ephesus, center of the Greek world in Asia Minor, to have to consult Syrian courtiers before writing an epitaph on one Antiochus of the small Asia Minor principality of Kommagini seems an odd circumstance, one that could point to the possibility of irony. Cavafy's use of the unusual term "Ἑλληνικός" (which in Modern Greek normally means "Greek" or—as Beaton puts it—"pertaining to Greece or Hellenism" and in ancient Greek anything from "Hellenic" and "Greek" to "like the Greeks," and "pure Greek," and "pagan"),[33] to describe the king's most precious quality of Hellenism also could be seen to promote an ironic reading. I quote the whole of the Ephesian sophist's epitaph in the Keeley-Sherrard version:

"People of Kommagini, let the glory of Antiochus,
the noble king, be celebrated as it deserves.
He was a provident ruler of the country.
He was just, wise, courageous.
In addition he was that best of all things, Hellenic—
mankind has no quality more precious:
everything beyond that belongs to the gods."

[32] The phrase was first applied to Cavafy by Francis Golffing in his essay "The Alexandrian Mind: Notes Toward a Definition," *Partisan Review* (Winter, 1955), p. 76.

[33] See Liddell and Scott, "Ἑλληνικός."

Beaton tells us that "the epitaph records a historical accident, not an ideological commitment," and he sees the unusual term "Hellenic" serving two purposes, neither of which is ironic: it confers on the dead king the kind of praise he would have most appreciated as an educated man of his time, namely "belonging to Hellenism," and it does so with the kind of exemplary modesty that most befits the gentle and cultured Antiochus. So the irony of the poem does not lie in the epitaph but in its having been "suggested as appropriate to the occasion by Syrian courtiers." Beaton concludes:

> . . . the epitaph with its subtle modesty and glorification of Hellenism is not the spontaneous, unaided work of the Greek sophist called in to write it. At one level of irony this undermines the whole epitaph, so that its purpose is merely to flatter and the sentiments expressed no more than the current fashion at an obscure middle-eastern court. But at the same time the irony also serves to deepen the meaning of "Hellenism" in the poem and show the essential contradiction at its heart: that what is called "Hellenic" and praised so highly is as much the creation of Syrians and others as of Greeks.[34]

Taken outside the Cavafian context, one might not quarrel with this analysis. But serious questions remain regarding the poet's attitude toward his material and the perspective that finally emerges from the poem. With respect to the first "level of irony" as described above, is it among Cavafy's intentions to satirize this "obscure middle-eastern court" with its cultured, gentle, just, wise, courageous, and provident ruler but its presumably sycophantic and trendy Syrian courtiers, given to post-mortem flattery and fashion-mongering?[35] That would

[34] "Cavafy," p. 525.
[35] Though Beaton tells us that Cavafy did not use irony "to debunk certain attitudes and characters," what other implication can one draw from Beaton's view that one level of the poet's irony "undermines the whole epitaph" so that we see that "its purpose is merely to flatter and the sentiments expressed no more than the current fashion at an obscure middle-eastern court"? But

seem, on one level, too easy a mark for Cavafy and, on another level, quite out of key with both the image we are given of Antiochus and the poet's persistent image of Syria and Syrians. And Beaton's second level of irony, the one that serves to "show the essential contradiction at the poem's heart," namely that what is called "Hellenic" and highly praised "is as much the creation of Syrians and others as of Greeks," raises a related question. Is the implication of the poet's supposed irony at this level that a Hellenism which is in part the creation of Syrians (most likely once citizens of Antioch, Beirut, or Selefkia, Cavafy's principal Syrian cities) cannot be truly Hellenic nor represent a quality that the epitaph calls mankind's highest or most precious? This is hardly an implication that those familiar with Cavafy's treatment of diaspora Hellenism in poem after poem, over a priod of some twenty-five years, are likely to accept. Is it the poet's irony at the expense of "Syrians and others," his showing the contradiction occasioned by non-Hellenes contributing to Hellenism, that deepens the meaning of the concept in the poem? Or is it his specifically identifying their contribution—their quite valid, noncontradictory contribution—and by implication his celebrating of it that serves to deepen the meaning of Hellenism and establish the particular appropriateness of the term "Hellenic"?

The point of the poem is that of course Syrian courtiers, and Syrian courtiers perhaps most of all, would be able to advise on an epitaph in which the unusual term "Hellenic," as Cavafy meant it, plays such a significant role. Are not these Syrian courtiers from that part of the world that is constantly identified as among the centers of diaspora Hellenism in Cavafy, especially during the historical period encompassed by the poem (his editor George Savidis tells us that this Antiochus "could be any one of several kings of the same name who reigned in Kommagini between 64 B.C. and A.D. 72)? Three

since neither he nor Vayenas actually defines irony, I may be missing some new sense of the term that is not encompassed by standard definitions, e.g., that in *Encyclopedia of Poetry and Poetics*, pp. 407-408.

other poems that Beaton discusses in his essay show Syria to be a primary source of Hellenism during this period, in particular the kind of diaspora Hellenism that is designated by the term "Hellenic" and that Cavafy is reported by both Stratis Tsirkas and Timos Malanos to have claimed as his own: "I too am Hellenic (Ἑλληνικός). Notice how I put it: not Greek (Ἕλλην), nor Hellenized (Ἑλληνίζων), but Hellenic (Ἑλληνικός)." This remark, apparently first offered by Cavafy in conversation with Tsirkas,[36] comes in so pat against irony and satire in this instance that Beaton has to work his way around it by a curious, unsubstantiated argument that seems to me to let him have his cake and eat it too: he dismisses "the evident identity of sympathy between Cavafy and his character in this poem" that the remark appears to reinforce by telling us that the remark "was not intended for publication," and, in any case, "an essential and courageous feature of Cavafy's irony is that it spares neither himself nor his predilections" (p. 525, n. 22). Sometimes so indeed,[37] but where are the grounds for assuming such self-irony, and the distance it implies, in this instance?

But along with the "biographical" gloss provided by the remark to Tsirkas, we have the gloss provided by the three poems themselves. In "Returning from Greece" (or, as Diskin Clay has shrewdly suggested, "Going Home from Greece"[38] or "Homeward Bound from Greece"), the philosopher-speaker, who identifies himself as a diaspora Greek returning to his home waters of Cyprus, Syria, and Egypt, tells us that the correct attitude for "Greeks like us" is to honor and delight in "the Syrian and Egyptian blood in our veins"—in other words, to honor that quality of being "Hellenic" as distinct from that quality represented by mainland Greeks (without

---

[36] And reported by Timos Malanos in Περί Καβάφη (Alexandria, 1935), p. 56.

[37] As I myself indicate in my comments on "In the Year 200 B. C.," Cavafy's Alexandria, pp. 145-148.

[38] See "The Silence of Hermippos: Greece in the Poetry of Cavafy," Byzantine and Modern Greek Studies, No. 3 (1977), p. 109.

"Asiatic tastes and feelings") or that quality represented by pretenders to Hellenism, with their "showy Hellenified exteriors" based on a Macedonian model.[39] The Syrian courtiers of "Epitaph of Antiochus . . ." are not identified specifically as Greeks from Syria, though they could be: as we see in "One of Their Gods," Greeks from Syria are taken to be what we would now call native Syrians, distinguished in the poem from a "stranger" or "foreigner" (ξένος) in Syrian Selefkia. They are in any case very much a part of the mixture—the "κρᾶμα"[40] that constitutes the essence of Cavafy's diaspora "Hellenic" world. And in "Herodis Attikos," which presents this Hellenic world in the second century after Christ, the speaker describes Alexander of Selefkia in Syria as "one of our better sophists," and he tells us that at this time "future orators" being trained by Hellenism are getting their training in the two Syrian cities of Beirut and Antioch (as well as Alexandria).[41] Finally, such

[39] In his note to the poem, *Cavafy: Collected Poems*, p. 434, Savidis suggests that the poem's "Hermippos" may be the grammarian of the time of Trajan and Hadrian (A.D. 98-138), but the time of the poem's discourse has to remain speculative.

[40] The term comes from "In a Town of Osroini."

[41] Beaton gives this poem an interesting reading, but he fails to establish sufficient distinction between the poet and his speaker. The poem is a dramatic monologue, and the speaker, when he calls Alexander of Selefkia "one of our better sophists," identifies himself as a Greek of the diaspora. He is thus limited in his point of view by both the particular historical context and the implications of his diaspora "hellenic" identity. I have two specific quibbles. What Beaton sees as the poet's irony at Herodis's expense is based on Herodis supposedly being "content, as it appears he is, to enjoy his 'luck' and to be 'followed only.' " Herodis may or may not have been content to enjoy his "luck." The speaker simply tells us that "tactful" (λεπτός) Herodis answers the sophist Alexander by saying that instead of sending the Greeks back to Athens to hear Alexander speak, Herodis will return with them, presumably because they will not return without him. And it is the diaspora speaker, observing the scene from the perspective of someone living in Alexandria, Antioch, or Beirut, who offers the expression "the Greeks (the Greeks!)." Beaton tells us that the repetition "implies not admiration but incredulity." The repetition does indeed suggest incredulity on the speaker's part, but it also suggests thereby his implicit admiration for the Athenians in that the Athenians of the speaker's day (not of the classical past, because the poem

dubious Hellenism as the petty Asian monarch of "Philhellene" can claim comes—if at all—from Syrian sophists.

Given this essential Cavafian context, it is not only difficult to envision the Syrian courtiers in "Epitaph of Antiochus . . ." as the object of the poet's irony, but what Beaton sees as a contradiction at the poem's heart, "that what is called 'Hellenic' and praised so highly is as much the creation of Syrians and others as of Greeks" is, in the Cavafian context, no contradiction at all. The term "Hellenic" (Ἑλληνικός) as distinct from "Greek" or "Hellene" or "Philhellene" or "Hellenified non-Greek," aptly designates what Antiochus of the small Asia Minor principality of Kommagini would have felt himself to be and would have been honored to have himself designated in his epitaph, as Cavafy himself might have in keeping with his identification of himself as "Ἑλληνικός." And it is Syrian courtiers perhaps even more that a Greek sophist from Ephesus (which, as Beaton points out, though in Asia Minor "had been close [in this context, read too close] to the centre of the Greek world since pre-classical times") who would be most likely to understand the particular relevance of the term. Cavafy's friend and early critic, E. M. Forster, puts the case most

nowhere indicates that the *speaker* is interested in "the Greeks of the classical golden age, and of the classics textbooks") are depicted by him as having abandoned—at least in the presence of Herodis—their assumed superior capacity for disputations, for criticism and debate, since they apparently follow Herodis without criticism, debate, or even choice. So, in any case, the speaker pictures them, and without a recognition of his lingering admiration for the Athenians and without a sense of the possible distance between poet and speaker in this respect, the reader has little basis for discovering the poet's irony regarding the decline of Athenian sophistry. In a note that appears in Ὁ Καβάφης ἀπαραμόρφωτος (Athens, 1981, pp. 85-86, originally published as a letter to the editor in *Kathimerini*), Timos Malanos informs us that in this poem Cavafy uses the repeated term Ἕλληνες (the Greeks) with "anything but the local meaning." His meaning, according to Malanos, is derived from his source, Philostratos's *Lives of the Sophists*, where the term "does not mean a resident of Greece or the Greek in general, but exclusively and only 'the student of rhetoric.' " Malanos bases his view of what Philostratos means by the term on the Glossary to the Loeb edition of Philostratos, trans. W. C. Wright (Cambridge, Mass. and London, 1922), p. 569.

succinctly: "[Cavafy] was a loyal Greek, but Greece for him was not territorial. It was rather the influence that has flowed from his race this way and that through the ages, and that (since Alexander the Great) never disdained to mix with barbarism, has indeed desired to mix. . . . Racial purity bored him. . . . The civilization he respected was a bastardy in which the Greek strain prevailed, and into which, age after age, ousiders would push, to modify and be modified."[42]

Antiochus's epitaph does not celebrate the racially pure Hellenism associated with Classical Greece, that which is normally indicated by the term "Ἕλλην" (Greek or Hellene), but the specifically mixed Hellenism of diaspora Greece that includes "Asiatic tastes and feelings" which—as the Syrian-Egyptian philosopher of "Returning from Greece" suggested—are sometimes alien to Hellenism of the mainland Greek tradition and which, in the case of this philosopher, become the source of proper self-recognition and pride. In short, the "Ἑλληνικός" version of Hellenism is what Syrian courtiers in Kommagini would justly promote as mankind's highest quality. And that is why the poet has the Ephesian sophist and his Syrian advisers use that unusual, that special, term to honor the provident, wise, and courageous king of Kommagini. Neither he nor his courtiers are the object of the poet's irony. If there is irony in this poem too, it is directed at those who might choose to think that what the epitaph designates as mankind's highest quality is the exclusive province of "racially pure" Greeks belonging to the pre-Alexandrian tradition or their disciples, those who might find Cavafy's term "Ἑλληνικός" merely strange or confusing or ironic rather than special and therefore to the point.

In arriving at this not-so-ironic view of "Epitaph of Antiochus . . . ," one lays oneself open to two charges: that the reading is not sufficiently complicated (therefore presumably a bit old-fashioned if not downright naive) and that it draws

---

[42] *Two Cheers for Democracy* (London, 1951), pp. 249-250. Forster's essay on Cavafy was omitted from the American edition of this collection.

for some of its implications not simply on the text under perusal but also on a "structure" of attitudes created by other Cavafy poems presumed to be relevant, in this case specifically those that are seen to build a complex and special image of Hellenism. Regarding the first charge, I personally find sufficient complication and richness in Cavafy for my taste even when his irony is muted, and though I am willing to admit to being a bit old-fashioned—a reformed New Critic, if you will—I would hope that my approach is not naive. Also, given my view of Cavafy's work both here and in the past, I plead guilty to the second charge as well, and to the further charge of believing that though Cavafy was a consummate ironist, he nevertheless did have certain convictions, and if not what is called a world-view, at least a perspective on the world that was complex, subtle, subject to development over the course of his career, yet generally identifiable. In fact, without some sense of this perspective as it developed over the years, it is almost impossible to establish the sources and implications of the poet's irony in specific instances, especially in the more complicated poems of his late years. Finally, I have to admit to seeing a certain structure in the images that Cavafy created of both ancient and modern Alexandria and of the broader world of Hellenism which most interested him, a structure that I have perhaps loosely called his "myth."[43] This is not the product of an attempt to discover a "hidden meaning" in Cavafy, nor to "decode" him in a particular way, nor to establish "ultimate, profound truth" outside the dramatic context of his work, as Beaton would have it.[44] The "myth" is a way of characterizing certain facets of what Beaton calls Cavafy's "autonomous dramatic world," this characterization for the purpose of illustrating the interrelation of many of his poems, which in turn is meant to help illuminate individual poems (what I presumed to be the function of criticism at the start of this discourse).

[43] The term, as I use it in *Cavafy's Alexandria*, is defined in particular on pp. 100-102.
[44] "Cavafy," pp. 517, 519, and 528.

I am grateful to both Nasos Vayenas and Roderick Beaton for the assistance their approach has given me in reinterpreting certain of the poems they have analyzed with new insight, but I cannot accept Vayenas's view that the "problem" of Cavafy's poetry is solved by looking simply at his use of irony, nor Beaton's view that irony is "all-pervasive in Cavafy's poetry," that "nothing in his poetic world is sacred," and that this world is entirely one of "shifting relativities." Though irony is central to Cavafy's work, it is not the only mode, and in his as in any other poetic world, the presence of irony depends on context. In Cavafy the context that helps the reader to determine exactly what may be subject to irony, and the degree to which irony may or may not be relevant, consists of many things: the poet's historical sources, the pattern of images and "structure" of attitudes that his poems build beyond his "shifting relativities," the tone and perspective—to invoke Auden again—that characterize his mature voice, and even the old-fashioned resources of the poet's biography and the poet's expression of attitudes outside his work.

At the risk of seeming to plead a personal case, I would again underline what Seferis identified as the virtue of reading Cavafy whole, of seeing his poetry as a life-long work-in-progress,[45] of studying the interrelation of his poems and the expanding perspective they shaped over the course of his career. But I have argued this at length elsewhere.[46] And for the disciple of New Criticism (however reformed), no definition or argument in the abstract has true substance outside its illustration through the analysis of specific texts.

[45] *On the Greek Style*, p. 125.

[46] I have in mind in particular the discussion of the advantages that may accompany the reader's awareness of the "myth in progress" that the poet built over a span of years, *Cavafy's Alexandria*, p. 148; and the discussion of the perspective that was made possible by "the unique mode of his mature poems," ibid., pp. 150-151.

SIKELIANOS:
THE SUBLIME VOICE

R eaders of contemporary Western poetry in the English-speaking world are usually familiar with the work of C. P. Cavafy and George Seferis to some degree and of Odysseus Elytis and Yannis Ritsos to a lesser degree, but very few have read Angelos Sikelianos (1884-1951), the poet who was next in importance to Cavafy in establishing the demotic tradition during the first half of this century and who was considered by Seferis to be equivalent in stature within that tradition to Yeats within ours. My principal concern here is with Sikelianos's late and, to my mind, his best poems, but given the general lack of access to him in the original outside Greece and the strictly selected character of English translations,[1] the English-speaking reader can have little sense of the range of his career. It may be useful, therefore, for me to set his late poems against the background out of which they emerged, that is, the sources that shaped him and the several early voices that were eventually transformed into the major voice that we hear at moments during the last two decades of his life.

[1] *Six Poets of Modern Greece*, trans. Edmund Keeley and Philip Sherrard (London, 1960 and New York, 1961) offered an early selection now out of print. More recent selections include those in *Modern Greek Poetry*, trans. Kimon Friar (New York, 1973); *Angelos Sikelianos: Selected Poems*, trans. Edmund Keeley and Philip Sherrard (Princeton and London, 1979); and *The Dark Crystal*, trans. Edmund Keeley and Philip Sherrard (Athens, 1981), published in the United States as *Voices of Modern Greece* (Princeton, 1981).

Sikelianos is a traditional poet in both the craft and thought that he gave his art, even more so perhaps than Cavafy, who was twenty years his senior, and Seferis, who was fewer years his junior. And that aspect of the Greek tradition that nourished Sikelianos is rather different from what English-speaking readers of Cavafy and Seferis are likely to expect. Sikelianos's work is rooted neither in the Hellenistic world of the diaspora that provided the principal historical context for Cavafy's poetic myth, nor in the Homeric and Platonic worlds that sustained Seferis's imagination, among other sources. Sikelianos drew his inspiration primarily from the pre-Socratic tradition, with Orphism and the cult of Dionysus, the teaching of Pythagoras, the Mysteries of Eleusis, and the mantic center at Delphi four of the main influences from this tradition. As Philip Sherrard has pointed out,[2] in these sources Sikelianos found a shared perspective that proclaimed not only the brotherhood of all men but of all living creatures and that placed man as the channel of communication between higher and lower states of existence, between the visible and the invisible. The pre-Socratic tradition also gave the poet his highest calling, that of inspired prophet and seer, of teacher and mystagogue, a calling that Sikelianos himself aspired to in modern Greece, as he believed Pindar and Aeschylus had in the classical period and as perhaps Wallace Stevens, in our day, would have understood with the largest sympathy since he gave poets the title "priests of the invisible."

Sikelianos saw the poet exercising the role of priest and seer largely through the agency of myth, in the sense that Schelling defined the term, that is, myth not as a fabrication but as a revelation of divine truth, a revelation of what is universal and timeless, with gods seen not merely as symbols but as living beings. We have ample evidence of Sikelianos's preoccupation with myth in this sense from his earliest work through the late period that most interests us here; yet, however much he may have been concerned with the representation of eternal

---

[2] *Review of National Literatures* (Fall, 1974), p. 100.

mysteries, of a universe where the ancient gods still survived palpably, his starting point in the best of his early poems was the natural world around him and the life of the senses that nourished his humanity. The natural world was for him inevitably a Greek world, both in its physical configuration and in its embodiment of traditional folk elements. And the poet who brings the gods to life in this natural world is a man of flesh and blood with the rhetoric characteristic of his people when touched by that passionate, sublime sense of something deeply interfused that rolls through all things (as Wordsworth put it):[3]

> The sun set over Acrocorinth
> burning the rock red. From the sea
> a fragrant smell of seaweed now began
> to intoxicate my slender stallion.
>
> Foam on the bit, the white of his eye
> bared fully, he struggled to break
> my grip, tight on the reins,
> to leap free into open space.
>
> Was it the hour? The rich odors?
> Was it the sea's deep saltiness?
> The forest's breathing far away?
>
> O had the meltemi held strong
> a little longer, I would have gripped
> the reins and flanks of mythic Pegasus!
>   ("On Acrocorinth")[4]

When Pan, in the early poem of that title, suddenly rises up over the burning heat of harsh pebbles on the shore opposite contemporary Salamis, the poet, in his easy passing between the world of flesh and the world of divinities, captures

---

[3] In "Lines Composed a Few Miles above Tintern Abbey."

[4] Translations of Sikelianos in this essay are from *Sikelianos: Selected Poems.* See that volume for relevant notes, e.g., on "meltemi."

the god's vitality by focusing on the majesty of his goatish form:

> Then we saw the herd's lord and master, the he-goat
>   rise alone
> and move off, hoof-beats slow and heavy,
>   toward a rock
>
> wedged into the sea to shape a perfect lookout point;
>   there he stopped,
> on the very edge where spray dissolves,
>   and leaning motionless,
>
> upper lip pulled back so that his teeth shone,
>   he stood
> huge, erect, smelling the white-crested sea
>   until sunset.

Given Sikelianos's conception of the poet as seer, as agent for bringing into close communion the mortal and the divine, it is not surprising to find that his persona, the first-person voice which is the dominant one in his earlier poems, often seem larger than life, almost a force in nature that transcends humanity, anyway the voice for rhetoric that seems both inspired and on occasion, grandiloquent. The persona sometimes actually assumes the identity and style of a self-ordained hierophant, an ascetic who has been initiated into the mysteries of both Dionysus and Christ, a voice that can directly address the gods and even their grand earthly habitations, as in the following excerpts from "Hymn to Artemis Orthia":

> O Taygetus,
> bronze mountain,
> at last you receive me as an ascetic! . . .
>
> what new impulses
> nourished my untamable and silent strength,
>
> veil of the tumult on your five peaks
> where the snow was slowly thawing,

aerial cataracts
of the flowering oleander
on the escarpments,

dawning of the Doric Apollo
before my eyes,
O harsh sculptured form
on the red unsoftened bronze!

This hierophantic, rhapsodic voice is the one least accessible
to a contemporary Western sensibility, not only because that
sensibility has been trained in our time to question rhetoric
of almost any kind, but because the voice depends for cred-
ibility and vitality on the character of the language it offers,
on the resonances and surprises that Sikelianos's creative—
one could even say prototypical—use of demotic brings to the
Greek reader. When the voice succeeds in the original (and it
does not always), it is likely to fail in translation to some
degree. The early voices of Sikelianos that are more accessible
to the English-speaking reader, that better survive the dan-
gerous crossing from one language to another, are those of
the first person, sometimes overtly subjective persona cele-
brating the natural world around him and his union with it
(as in "The Return," "The First Rain," and "Thalero") or the
rituals of peasant life that still evoke a rich—if dying—folk
tradition (as in "The Village Wedding") and the poet's nar-
rative voice telling the miracle of Dante's birth or of a Doric
virgin's first embrace.[5] But the greatest voice of all, to my
mind, appears during the mid-thirties to mid-forties, begin-
ning some fifteen years after the latest of the poems I have
been quoting, a voice that brilliantly combines the subjective
and the narrative in those late poems that reveal Sikelianos's
sublime tragic vision.

There is evidence in the poems themselves that this vision
of the immediately pre-World War II years was influenced by
a personal crisis of some kind, one perhaps having to do in
part with the death of Sikelianos's attempt to revive Delphi

---

[5] See *Sikelianos: Selected Poems*, "The Mother of Dante" and "Doric."

as a cultural and educational center and his increasing sense
of alienation from his contemporaries, perhaps in part with
his separation from his first wife (Eva Palmer) and eventually
from his only son. It was in any case a crisis marked by
suffering, and the subsequent catharsis seems to have brought
the poet both a new humility and a renewed sense of mission.
There is also implicit evidence that this personal catharsis in
the years immediately before the war prepared Sikelianos to
understand and to dramatize his country's cruel fate early in
the German Occupation—dramatize it with the kind of pro-
phetic wisdom that makes "Agraphon" one of the major Greek
poems of this century. But "Daedalus" is the poem that first
gives us a clear insight into the poet's late tragic sense of life,
and it is in this poem that we discover the particular voice he
fashioned to express what he had come to understand. The
narrative focuses on Daedalus—the great artificer, model for
the poet—and Daedalus's persistence in the pursuit of a dream,
that is, the creation of wings that will raise him "above the
crowd, / above the waves that swallowed up his child, / above
even the frontiers of lament, to save / with his own soul the
soul of the world." It is a dream of creation that he holds to
despite the misrepresentation, the condemnation, of "men un-
tried by suffering" and "feeble and embittered women" who
call him a "harsh father" for keeping to his fearful course in
order to save his own pathetic life, though "his sun was near
its setting." The narrative voice shifts to the subjective in the
last stanza as the poet establishes his kinship with the tireless
artificer and his noble search for the impossible, for that "awe-
inspiring Art" which "the dull crowd" considers to be "the
mere bauble of an idle mind.":

But you, great father, father of all of us
who from our earliest years have seen that everything
lies in the grave's shadow and who, with words
or chisel, have struggled with all our spirit
to rise above this flesh-consuming rhythm:

                                            father,
since for us too the earth and the heavens are one
and our own thought is the world's hearth and center,
since we also say that earth may mingle with the stars
as a field's subsoil with its topsoil, so that the heavens too
may bring forth wheat:
                          father, at those times
when life's bitterness weighs with its full burden
on our hearts, and our strength can be roused no more by
        youth
but only by the Will, that stands watchful
even over the grave, because to It the sea
which hugs the drowned remorselessly is itself shallow,
and shallow too the earth where the dead sleep;
in the dawn hours, as still we struggle on,
while the living and the dead both lie in the same
dreamless or dream-laden slumber, do not stop
ascending in front of us, but climb always
with slow even wings the heavens of our Thought,
eternal Daedalus, Dawnstar of the Beyond.

The voice here, though essentially personal, is rather different from that of the rhapsodic first-person seer who inhabits much of Sikelianos's earlier verse. The poet is no longer the hierophant transmitting a godly message through priestly rhetoric; he allows the myth at the poem's center to have its own life through narrative exposition, then brings himself into the myth by analogy, sharing its significance, joining his own experience of suffering and commitment to its revelation, but holding his focus on what the myth has already established, so that the personal dimension does not overwhelm the metaphorical. As a result, the voice in this poem is both convincing and sublime, and it carries a new implication of humility.

A similar voice speaks in "The Sacred Way," among the very best of the prewar poems. The subjective element is there from the start as the poet alludes rather more directly to the personal crisis that was only implicit in the previous poem:

"Through the new wound that fate had opened in me . . ."
and "like one long sick when he first ventures forth / to milk
life from the outside world, I walked / alone at dusk. . . ."
But he quickly establishes a mythological framework for this
personal journey of the spirit by describing the sacred road
to Eleusis that is its setting, a road he sees as a river bearing
ox-drawn carts that are loaded with people who seem shades
of the dead. And in this setting his journey merges with that
of others taken centuries ago along the same road. Before the
metaphor becomes uncomfortably labored, the poet moves on
to his narrative about a gypsy and two dancing bears, and
though there are further allusions to Demeter, Alcmene, and
the Holy Virgin in support of the mythological framework,
the tragic sense of life at the heart of the poem emerges most
powerfully from the story that the poet tells of a mother bear
rising up in pain out of an ill-fated tenderness to dance vig-
orously so that her innocent child will be spared a premature
knowledge of the suffering that is his inevitable destiny:

> And then, as they drew near to me, the gypsy,
> before I'd really noticed him, saw me,
> took his tambourine down from his shoulder,
> struck it with one hand, and with the other tugged
> fiercely at the chains. And the two bears
> rose on their hind legs heavily. One of them,
> the larger—clearly she was the mother—
> her head adorned with tassels of blue beads
> crowned by a white amulet, towered up
> suddenly enormous, as if she were
> the primordial image of the Great Goddess,
> the Eternal Mother, sacred in her affliction,
> who, in human form, was called Demeter
> here at Eleusis, where she mourned her daughter,
> and elsewhere, where she mourned her son,
> was called Alcmene or the Holy Virgin.
> And the small bear at her side, like a big toy,
> like an innocent child, also rose up, submissive,

not sensing yet the years of pain ahead
or the bitterness of slavery mirrored
in the burning eyes his mother turned on him.

But because she, dead tired, was slow to dance,
the gypsy, with a single dexterous jerk
of the chain hanging from the young bear's nostril—
bloody still from the ring that had pierced it
perhaps a few days before—made the mother,
groaning with pain, abruptly straighten up
and then, her head turning toward her child,
dance vigorously.

It is through this convincingly narrated action that the poet
earns our assent to the mother bear's mythic role as "huge
testifying symbol / of all primaeval suffering for which, /
throughout the human centuries, the soul's / tax has still not
been paid. Because the soul / has been and still is in Hell."
And it is through the carefully plotted merging of the narrative
and personal elements, of the mythical figure as eternal suf-
ferer and the persona as "slave to this world," that the poet
persuades us to accept both the tragic implications of the poem
and the tentative resolution that concludes it:

Then, as the gypsy
at last went on his way, again dragging
the slow-footed bears behind him, and vanished
in the dusk, my heart prompted me once more
to take the road that terminates among
the ruins of the Soul's temple, at Eleusis.
And as I walked my heart asked in anguish:
"Will the time, the moment ever come when the bear's soul
and the gypsy's and my own, that I call initiated,
will feast together?"
                              And as I moved on, night fell,
and again through the wound that fate had opened in me
I felt the darkness flood my heart as water

pours through a hole in a sinking ship.
Yet when—as though it has been thirsting for that flood—
my heart sank down completely into the darkness,
sank completely as though to drown in the darkness,
a murmur spread through all the air above me,
a murmur,
                    and it seemed to say:
                              "It will come."

The poem "Agraphon," written during the devastating
Athenian autumn of 1941 under the German Occupation, is
the purest example of Sikelianos's late mode. Two-thirds of
the poem consists of a narrated parable that is offered without
introduction, except that which is implied by the title: a saying
or tradition about Christ not recorded in the Gospels or ca-
pable of being traced to its original source. The parable tells
a story of corruption outside the walls of Zion that Jesus,
walking with his disciples, sees as a metaphor for corruption
inside the city; but more important, He finds within the cor-
ruption, represented literally by a dog's stinking carcass, the
glitter of white teeth "like hailstones, like a lily, beyond decay,
/ a great pledge, mirror of the Eternal, but also / the harsh
lightning-flash, the hope of Justice." The parable is presented
as straight narrative, then the personal voice is heard for the
last third of the poem, not as a commentary on what has been
presented but as an assimilation of it into the poet's immediate
world, where the Zion of his time has become analogous to
that corrupt city which Christ knew, and where the tragic
circumstances enveloping the poet have brought him to that
final knowledge and humility which the ancient poets tell us
can come from intense suffering alone. The poet prays:

And now, Lord, I,
the very least of men, ponder your words,
and filled with one thought, I stand before you:
grant me, as now I walk outside this Zion,
and the world from end to end is all ruins, garbage,

all unburied corpses choking the sacred
springs of breath, inside and outside the city:
grant me, Lord, as I walk through this terrible stench,
one single moment of Your holy calm,
so that I, dispassionate, may also pause
among this carrion and with my own eyes
somewhere see a token, white as hailstones,
as the lily—something glittering suddenly
deep inside me, above the putrefaction,
beyond the world's decay, like the dog's teeth
at which that sunset You gazed, Lord, in wonder:
a great pledge, mirror of the Eternal, but also
the harsh lightning-flash, the hope of Justice!

The voice in this poem moves us perhaps as no other in
Sikelianos's verse not so much because the reality of that bitter
1941 season gives substance to his rhetoric, but because the
poet's prayer comes to us after he has narrated a story, a myth
in Schelling's sense, that provides both an objective and a
generalized context for his personal, his national, predica-
ment. Again, what there is of subjective rhetoric in the poem
becomes tranferred into the universal and the sublime.

During the period of the German Occupation, Sikelianos
wrote a number of poems that were a direct, uncomplicated,
unsubtle expression of his passionate concern for his country's
fate, poems meant to rouse the spirit of resistance and to
celebrate the heroic stance of his people. Overt rhetoric re-
turned in the nation's service. Every Greek schoolchild of the
period (including those of the Greek diaspora) still remembers
the opening lines of the famous poem Sikelianos recited over
the coffin of Kostis Palamas, his eminent predecessor, on Feb-
ruary 28, 1943:

Blow, bugles. . . . Thundering bells,
shake the whole country, from end to end . . .[6]

[6] From "Palamas" in Sikelianos's *Lyrical Life*, 5.

The recitation itself was an act of resistance, followed as it was by Sikelianos's booming voice rendering the forbidden Greek national anthem for the entertainment of the plain-clothed German occupiers who had come to mix, rather bewildered, with the huge crowd of mourners at Palamas's funeral. Now, so many years after the fact, one perhaps sees those lines on Palamas's death and other patriotic poems of the time as the least satisfactory manifestation of Sikelianos's late voice—that is, viewed from a strictly literary perspective. But what I want to emphasize in conclusion is that Sikelianos did in fact write one poem that successfully projected, through the agency of myth, both his passionate feeling for his country's fate—that harsh lightning-flash hope of Justice—and his more universal tragic sense of life. There are lines in "Agraphon" that I believe will long survive as poetry both in and beyond the context of their historical occasion and specifically national impulse. That accomplishment by itself demonstrates why Sikelianos is one of the truly great masters in the modern Greek tradition.

SIKELIANOS
AND GREEK MYTHOLOGY

In the introduction to *Angelos Sikelianos: Selected Poems*, the translators speak of Sikielanos's "mythological attitude ... toward life" (p. xiv) and of his conception of myth not so much "as a rhetorical or metaphorical device but as a spontaneous creation of the human soul directed toward the revelation of a hidden spiritual life" (p. xvii), in short, mythology seen as a kind of religion closely related to Schelling's perception of the function of myth. These remarks, offered in similar language some years ago,[1] may have their just proportion of truth, but in keeping with most introductory remarks, they strike me as rather too general, rather too undiscriminating when one brings them face to face with Sikelianos's practice at different moments of his career. I want to try to be more discriminating here by considering the role of myth—specifically ancient Greek myth—in the poet's work both early and late in his career. I think it is a changing role, perhaps not in his fundamental association of gods with a contemporary landscape and his revelation of those mysteries that lie hidden in our everyday lives, but in the mode of this association and this revelation, and in the depth of their poetic significance.

The first of the early poems most relevant to my theme is "The Horses of Achilles" (1909):[2]

---

[1] See the "Introduction" to *Six Poets of Modern Greece*, pp. 9ff.
[2] The translations in this essay are from *Sikelianos: Selected Poems*.

Field of asphodels, beside you
two horses neighed
as they went by at a gallop.
Their backs gleamed like a wave;
they came up out of the sea,
tore over the deserted sand,
necks straining high, towering,
white foam at the mouth, stallion-strong.
In their eyes
lightning smoldered;
and, waves themselves, they plunged again
into the waves,
foam into the sea's foam,
and vanished. I recognized
those stallions: one of them
took on a human voice to prophesy.
The hero held the reins;
he spurred, hurling
his godlike youth forward . . .

Sacred stallions, fate
has kept you indestructible,
fixing on your pure black foreheads,
charm against the profane eye,
a large and pure white talisman.

There is a wonderful innocence in the poet's handling of
the mythology in this poem. The horses are described in the
first instance as one might describe any gallant horses in the
field next door, except for a certain metaphoric heightening—
"their backs gleamed like a wave"—and a touch of heroic
diction such as "towering" and "stallion-strong," all prepar-
ing for the stated mystery of the lightning smoldering in their
eyes and their supernatural union with the natural world:
"waves themselves, they plunged again / into the waves, foam
into the sea's foam, / and vanished." But the poet does not

leave it at that; he goes on to tell us, charmingly, that he recognized those stallions named in the title of his poem, one of them known to be a prophet, and he even has the hero to whom they belong suddenly spur them on in his godlike way. And he concludes the movement from objective description to subjective accommodation by actually addressing the stallions in order to underline their immortality and their spiritual incorruptibility.

It is an uncomplicated evocation of the myth, perhaps too limited in its nuances when one compares it to Cavafy's relatively early poem of the same title. Cavafy's handling of the myth underlines not the rather obvious mystery of the horses' immortality and incorruptibility but their almost human compassion as they weep over the "eternal disaster of death" that they come to recognize as the lot of even heroic mortals when they find Patroklos dead. But if we accept Sikelianos's poem on its own terms, which are neither pretentious nor profound, it does serve through its rhetoric to bring new life into the myth.

A more subtle example of the same early mode is found in the poem "Aphrodite Rising" (1915), where the poet again restricts himself to an evocation of a well-known myth without any fundamental reinterpretation and only a limited extension of the myth's significance, but with the difference that in this instance he assumes a fully dramatic stance, and instead of bringing himself directly into the mythical context as commentator—not to say as master of ceremonies in the occasion of mystery—he allows the myth to speak for itself, almost literally, since the poem is a dramatic monologue with the goddess of love herself as speaker:

In the blessed rose light of dawn, look how I rise,
    my arms held high.
The sea's godlike calm bids me to ascend
    into the blue air.

O but the sudden breaths of earth, filling my breasts, rousing me
    from head to foot.
O Zeus, the sea is heavy, and my loosened hair drags me
    down like a stone.

Nymphs of the breeze, hurry; Kymothoe, Glafke, come grip me
    under the arms.
I did not think I'd find myself so suddenly caught up
    in the sun's embrace.

This poem is more in the late Cavafian mode than either
of the two poems called "The Horses of Achilles," partly
because it is a dramatic monologue, more important because
the significance of the poet's mythic evocation comes to us
not by way of the poet's subjective commentary but directly
out of the particular manner and substance of the evocation
itself, namely the wonderful tension in Sikelianos's goddess
between the impulse toward divine ascension and earthly hab-
itation, or to put it another way, the paradox of her emerging
godliness so overwhelmed by those sudden breaths of earth
that rouse her from head to foot and by the passion of her
being caught up in the sun's embrace beyond even divine
expectation.

Another early poem, "Pan" (1914), takes a middle ground
between the two modes we've explored so far. In this instance
the mythical context is established overtly by the title alone.
The opening stanzas of the poem could pass—in fact, do pass—
for a characteristic lyrical rendering of the contemporary Greek
landscape and seascape in the manner of those poems in Si-
kelianos that celebrate the natural world, especially as height-
ened by the poet's ecstatic response to what his eye sees and
his gut feels:

Over rocks on the deserted shore, over the burning heat
    of harsh pebbles,
beside the emerald waves, noon, like a fountain,
    rose shimmering.

Salamis a blue trireme deep in the sea,
      in spring's spindrift;
the pines and mastic trees of Kineta a deep breath
      I drew inside me.

The sea burst into foam and, beaten by the wind,
      shattered white,
and a flock of goats, countless, iron-gray, plummeted headlong
      down the hill.

But in the best early poems of Sikelianos, the natural world subtly serves as a mask for the supernatural world; the poet's heightened response derives in part from his premonition, then his conviction, that divinities are hiding behind the façade of earthly presences. In this instance, the flock of goats "plummet[ing] headlong" down the hillside soon becomes an occasion for that kind of mystery, namely the metamorphosis of the herd's lord and master into the god Pan, rising to face the sea as though some secret sun ritual has called him up out of the slumber of the ages:

They gathered in close, crowding the brush
      and wild thyme,
and as they gathered, a drowsiness seized
      both goats and man.

And then, over the shore's stones and the goat's swelter,
      dead silence;
and between their horns, as from a tripod, the sun's quick heat
      shimmered upward.

Then we saw the herd's lord and master, the he-goat,
      rise alone
and move off, his tread slow and heavy,
      toward a rock

wedged into the sea to shape a perfect lookout point;
      there he stopped,
on the very edge where spray dissolves,
      and leaning motionless,

upper lip pulled back so that his teeth shone,
    he stood
huge, erect, smelling the white-crested sea
    until sunset.

In this poem Sikelianos has moved from subjective respond-
ent to objective narrator. Again there is no overt commentary
on the mythical context that emerges; the unstated mystery
of Pan's apparition in the noonday heat on the shore between
Eleusis and Corinth is sufficient for his purpose because it
works dramatically, without need for underlining, to present
his case for our believing that the ancient pastoral gods are
still very much with us—or at least were as recently as the
1920s, when Kineta, currently a tourist beach, was still open
country for goats and their attendant herdsmen.

I turn now to Sikelianos's later work, in particular the poems
"Daedalus" and "The Sacred Way," both published during
the period immediately preceding World War II and after the
poet had apparently suffered a personal crisis that was re-
solved, at least as far as his work is concerned, by the emer-
gence of a new and powerful tragic vision.[3] These two poems
and several others of his late years reveal a depth of perception
that clearly transcends the personal lyricism and even the ac-
cess to mystery that established his strong reputation in earlier
years. And it is in some measure Sikelianos's fresh approach
to myth—ancient Greek myth in particular—that allowed his
broadened vision to find an effective voice. The new approach
can be described as the total assimilation of the myth by the
poet's point of view. The subjective element here is not that
of a poet addressing his mythic material so as to highlight it
or to comment on its vitality or even to personalize the mystery
in it in order to give it renewed life and to make it dramatically
contemporary, though aspects of these earlier modes are still
in evidence, are still brought into play by the poet when they
are needed to further his purpose. The subjective element has

[3] As is discussed in the preceding essay.

now become, more than anything else, the essential definition that the poet brings to the myth, his unembarrassed if sometimes complex statement of the wisdom he finds in it. And he also does not hesitate to impose whatever rhetorical pressure he feels his material should bear to make his interpretation of the myth, his insight into the meaning he finds there, a persuasive poetic act. In short, the approach is that of the seer, the inspired didact, presenting his mythological lesson in a manner intended to capture our hearts as well as our minds. The dominant tone—and it is a tone characteristic of much of the best of Sikelianos's late work—sounds clearly at the start of the poem entitled "Daedalus":

> The fate of Icarus could have been no other
> than to fly and to perish . . . Because when he put on
> freedom's awe-inspiring wings, their equipoise the art
> of his great father, it was youth alone
> that flung his body into danger, even if
> he also failed, perhaps, to find their secret balance.

That, in so many words, is the meaning of Icarus's fate: given his youth, he could not have done other than he did; the necessary impulse of his young blood is what took him too close to the sun. And with this quick view of the mythical figure who has so often moved the poetic imagination and even here occasions the lamentation of men "untried by suffering," Sikelianos settles that aspect of his myth's mystery and turns to the aspect which really interests him, namely the meaning of the "great father's" fate, that of the sleepless artificer, Daedalus. Sikelianos's focus becomes what one might call the reverse side of the coin that Auden examines in his famous poem of the same period, "Musée des Beaux Arts."[4]

---

[4] Auden's poem, written in early 1939 and published in 1940 (see Edward Mendelson, *Early Auden*, New York, 1981, pp. 361-362), is contemporary with Sikelianos's, which was first published in the June 15, 1938 issue of *Nea Estia* (see G. K. Katsimbalis, *Bibliography of A. Sikelianos*, Athens, 1971). In 1943 Sikelianos published a verse drama entitled *Daedalus in Crete*,

Auden's message is that the masters who best depicted moments of mystery—"the miraculous birth," "the dreadful martyrdom"—always juxtaposed the mystery with moments of ordinary unmysterious life, the doggy life that has the torturer's horse "scratching its innocent behind on a tree," or in the case of Breughel's *Icarus*, has everything turning away leisurely from the disaster, including the "expensive delicate ship" that sails calmly on despite the amazing thing it has seen: a boy falling out of the sky. In short, Auden emphasizes how well the Old Masters understood the *human* position of suffering. Sikelianos on the other hand emphasizes the superhuman position of suffering and the danger of misapprehension that lies in too much concern for the merely human. As we have seen, those who give way to an excess of lamentation over Icarus's necessary fate are called "untried by suffering," as are those, along with their feeble women, who call the father Daedalus harsh, or self-serving, or a man in pursuit of the impossible, presumably for having devised wings which would lead to his son's death at the same time that a second set brought Daedalus his own freedom. Contrary to the lamenters, the feeble of heart, and the undiscerning, Sikelianos sees in Daedalus not only the supremely dedicated artist who carries his grand work forward even when those around him consider it "the mere bauble of an idle mind," but Christlike in his mission to rise above "this flesh-consuming rhythm," above the crowd, the waves, even the frontiers of lament in order to "save with his own soul of the world." It is a difficult message to transmit, but in one of those mysterious ways that poetry sometimes moves, Sikelianos brings it off, perhaps first of all because he manages successfully to personalize the myth's teaching without banality, and, more important, because he courageously allows his voice to assume a grand style appropriate to the grandeur of his conviction (even if the translated voice I offer here must be taken for an approximation at best,

---

the last expression of what George Savidis tells me was a lifelong preoccupation on the poet's part with the dramatic possibilities of the Daedalus-Icarus myth, one that began c. 1905.

though I might add that the style depends for its effect more
on rhythmic momentum than diction):

                                                    father,
since for us too the earth and the heavens are one
and our own thought is the world's hearth and center,
since we also say that earth may mingle with the stars
as a field's subsoil with its topsoil, so that the heavens too
may bring forth wheat: father, at those times
when life's bitterness weighs with its full burden
on our hearts, and our strength can be roused no more by youth
but only by the Will that stands watchful
even over the grave, because to It the sea
which hugs the drowned remorselessly is itself shallow,
and shallow too the earth where the dead sleep;

in the dawn hours, as still we struggle on,
while the living and the dead both lie in the same
dreamless or dream-laden slumber, do not stop
ascending in front of us, but climb always
with slow even wings the heavens of our Thought,
eternal Daedalus, Dawnstar of the Beyond.

Since "The Sacred Way" is among Sikelianos's best known
and most discussed poems (that is, within the small circle that
discusses Sikelianos at all), only a few remarks are called for
here.[5] In terms of our theme, the poem should be identified
as the most original manifestation of the progress I have been
outlining. What happens in this poem is another version of
the kind of assimilation and personalization of ancient sources
that we saw in "Daedalus," and even beyond that, an attempt
on the poet's part to create his own myth in the image of his
ancient ancestors. The poet begins his spiritual journey in this
poem by setting out from Athens on the road that leads to
the home of the Eleusinian Mysteries—an avenue that he tells
us he has always looked upon as "the Soul's road." And the
roadside rock he chooses to rest on in his journey seems to

---

[5] For further comments on the poem, see above, Sik. 1.

him "like a throne / long predestined for me," so that when he settles on it he forgets if "it was today that I'd set out or if / I'd taken this road centuries before." The ground is thus fully prepared for the mythical dimension that the poet brings to the tale that follows, the little mystery play involving a passing gypsy and his two dancing bears, mother and child, the mother bear enormous enough to seem, in the poet's words, the Great Goddess, the Eternal Mother. And when we are shown her rising up in her immense weariness to dance vigorously because she sees the gypsy tug cruelly at the wound in her child's nostril, this touchingly human gesture on her part can become—given the mythical context that the poet has cunningly established—something of a ritual act that transforms the mother bear into a "huge testifying symbol / of all primaeval suffering for which, / throughout the human centuries, the soul's / tax has still not been paid. Because the soul / has been and still is in Hell." And our assent to this gesture and the meaning given it permits us to accept the poet's own sudden humility, even the whispered conviction, the affirmation, that ends the poem as the poet's question: "Will the time, the moment ever come when the bear's soul / and the gypsy's and my own, that I call initiated, / will feast together?" finds an answer from the voice of mystery: "It will come."

The poem is one of Sikelianos's very finest, and so is "Daedalus." That is what permits me to speak of a progress in the poet's use of ancient Greek sources. It is always convenient for the structure of a critic's argument to see a poet getting better as he moves from youth to maturity to old age, but of course this is hardly always the case; one thinks of great poets who could not carry us the whole distance without ending up dissatisfying us beyond reasonable expectation: Wordsworth and Browning, for example. But like Yeats in the English tradition and Cavafy in the Greek tradition, Sikelianos did produce some of his finest work in his later years, and his growth to the status of major poet is demonstrated, I think, in at least some measure by the progress in his use of myth that I have tried to illustrate here.

SEFERIS'S ELPENOR:
A MAN OF NO FORTUNE

For the poet who draws on classical mythology in shaping the drama of his verse, there is an advantage to being Greek. Unlike his contemporaries in England or America, the Greek poet can evoke characters and settings that have mythological overtones without danger of being merely literary in doing so, without danger of arbitrarily imposing gods and heroes on an alien landscape—Tiresias on the Thames or Prometheus in Pennsylvania, for example. As anyone who has visited Greece knows, the gods and heroes of Homer's world confront the mind's eye as constantly and plausibly as the whitewashed huts or broad-beamed caiques that one actually sees; the mythology survives as a palpable reality in the road sign to the town or village one has chosen to explore, in the acropolis or temple or not so innocent mound of stones on the hillside opposite the hotel, in the waiter's classical rather than Christian name.

George Seferis is the contemporary Greek poet who has perhaps made the most of his advantage in being Greek.[1] His poetry fully exploits the survival of mythic gods and heroes in the landscape of modern Greece, and it does so as naturally, as unpretentiously, as one would expect in a poet of genius—much in the manner of Yeats's best mythological verse, where Irish (and even non-Irish) heroes move into a contemporary scene with the ease of Shakespeare's ghosts. Seferis's secret (in addition to his advantage) is that he usually offers an

[1] In this connection, see also "Sikelianos and Greek Mythology" above, and "Elytis and the Greek Tradition" below.

appropriate setting—a poetically realistic setting—when he has his local ghosts appear on his stage; as he attempts to carry the reader to the level of myth, the level of timeless universalities, he wins his sympathy and belief by convincingly representing the present reality sustaining his myth—a contemporary, Greek reality always:

> Three rocks, a few burnt pines, a solitary chapel
> and farther above
> the same landscape repeated starts again
> three rocks in the shape of a gate-way, rusted,
> a few burnt pines, black and yellow,
> and a square hut buried in whitewash;
> and still farther above, many times over,
> the same landscape recurs level after level
> to the horizon, to the twilight sky.
>
> Here we moored the ship to splice the broken oars
> to drink water and to sleep.
> The sea that embittered us is deep and unexplored
> and unfolds a boundless calm.
> Here among the pebbles we found a coin
> and threw dice for it.
> The youngest won it and disappeared.
>
> We set out again with our broken oars.[2]

The landscape depicted in the first stanza of this poem, No. 12 from the group appropriately entitled *Mythistorima*,[3] is as contemporary and as representative as any one might come across on a caique or other ship cruising the Aegean. Its solitary chapel, hut buried in whitewash, and scattered burnt pines are first of all literal: such is the arid, rocky, virtually

---

[2] Translations of Seferis's poetry in this and subsequent essays, unless otherwise indicated, are from *George Seferis: Collected Poems*, trans. Edmund Keeley and Philip Sherrard (Princeton, 1981).

[3] For the poet's note on the title and further discussion of it, see Sef. 2, below.

uninhabited prospect that many Greek shores offer the con-
temporary traveler. It is not until the second stanza, after we
have absorbed the literalness, the reality, of this landscape,
that its symbolic and mythic implications are dramatized: we
discover that the travelers looking up at this contemporary
setting are no ordinary travelers passing by on a steamship,
but the ghosts of Odysseus and his companions mooring their
black-hulled galley to mend broken oars. The myth suddenly
comes to life, the ancient and modern worlds meet in a met-
aphor without strain or contrivance, the timeless dimension
of the present is suddenly illuminated as we see the Homeric
voyagers move anachronistically onto the contemporary stage
that the poet has set before our eyes.[4]

The anachronism is the whole point: in one sense, what
was then is now, and vice versa; the modern voyager shares
something of Odysseus's fate, while Odysseus finds a symbolic
representation of his fate in the modern setting that the poet
has him encounter: the deserted, arid, repetitious land and the
calm, embittering sea are symbolic of his frustrating voyage,
of his failure to realize the island paradise he longs for. And
his fate is that of every wanderer seeking a final harbor, a
spiritual fulfilment, that he can't seem to reach. The frustra-
tions of the wanderer are perennial; as Seferis puts it in an
illuminating comment on the role of mythic characters in his
verse: "men of inconstancy, of wanderings and of wars, though
they differ and may change in terms of greatness and value
. . . always move among the same monsters and the same
longings. So we keep the symbols and the names that the myth
has brought down to us, realizing as we do so that the typical
characters have changed in keeping with the passing of time
and the different conditions of our world—which are none
other than the conditions of everyone who seeks expression."[5]

---

[4] Cf. D. H. Lawrence's similar use of myth in *Last Poems*, a theme I explore
in "D. H. Lawrence's 'The Argonauts': Mediterranean Voyager with Crescent
Feet," *Deus Loci: The Lawrence Durrell Quarterly*, Vol. 5, No. 3 (March,
1982), pp. 9-13.

[5] From "A Letter on 'Thrush,'" *Anglohellenic Review*, Vol. 4, No. 12

The two mythological characters who are seen by the poet as the most representative of perennial attitudes appear in the poem quoted above. Odysseus—or "a certain Odysseus," to use Seferis's own terms[6]—is the poet's primary persona in *Mythistorima* (as he also is later in "*Thrush*"), more often than not, the first-person voice of the poem.[7] He speaks as a man who is striving for spiritual liberation but who finds his aspiration constantly frustrated by his weaker companions. The latter are represented by Elpenor, the youngest of the crew, who wins the coin at dice and typically disappears as the others set off again unpropitiously with the broken oars they apparently did not succeed in splicing. If the ghost of Odysseus is the principal narrator of Seferis's modern *Odyssey*, Elpenor is the principal subject of his narration: the typical "companion" on the voyage, the figure who reveals the weakness of spirit that so frustrates his captain and that makes the voyage agonizing and endless.

Several critics, the poet himself most significantly, have commented on the role of Odysseus in Seferis's verse; less attention has been given to Elpenor, a character as important in his way as the persona is in his, at least in those poems that reveal the maturest expression of the poet's mythology.[8]

(July-August, 1950), p. 501. Apparently at the poet's request, only a portion of this valuable essay was included in *On the Greek Style*. An English translation of the full text, with useful notes, by James Stone appeared in *Journal of the Hellenic Diaspora*, Vol. 7, No. 2 (Summer, 1980).

[6] "A Letter on '*Thrush*,' " p. 501.

[7] Orestes (in No. 16) and Andromache (in No. 17) are others. For a brief account of another of Seferis's personae, Stratis the Mariner (or Stratis Thalassinos) and his relation to Odysseus, see my essay, "George Seferis and Stratis the Mariner," *Accent* (Summer, 1956), pp. 153-157.

[8] Seferis's "A Letter on '*Thrush*' " is still the richest source for our understanding of the roles of both Odysseus and Elpenor. Helpful commentary may also be found in D. Nikolareizis, "The Presence of Homer in Modern Greek Poetry," *Nea Estia* (December, 1947) and "The Presence of Homer in the Poetry of George Seferis," *Anglohellenic Review*, Vol. 4 (January 1949-July 1950); in Vayenas, *The Poet and the Dancer*, pp. 271ff.; and in G. P. Savidis, *Metamorphoses of Elpenor (from Pound to Sinopoulos)* (Athens, 1981), pp. 15-22.

Elpenor is the figure who most clearly demonstrates Seferis's talent for making myth dramatic—that is, for representing the truths myth has to offer through characters in action. It is a talent that shows him to be close kin to Yeats, Pound, Eliot, D. H. Lawrence, and Robert Graves in the Anglo-American tradition, all of whom bring their mythic ghosts onto a precisely set stage for the rehearsal of some universally significant action. Pound actually invokes the figure of Elpenor to serve as one of his personae in the *Cantos*, offering an apt if highly personal tag for this Homeric subhero: "A man of no fortune, and with a name to come."

By "Homeric subhero" I mean that Elpenor is both a minor character in Homer and a man of little substance. His role in the *Odyssey* is limited to a few references and only one important scene. We learn at the end of Book X that he was the youngest of the companions, "no mainstay in a fight nor very clever,"[9] and that he broke his neck in a fall from Circe's roof after rising dazed from a night of too much wine, just before Odysseus sets out for his visit to the land of the dead. Elpenor appears on stage in Book XI as the first of the shades that Odysseus encounters in Hades:

One shade came first—Elpênor, of our company,
who lay unburied still on the wide earth
as we had left him—dead in Kirkê's hall,
untouched, unmourned, when other cares compelled us.
Now when I saw him there I wept for pity
and called out to him:
                    "How is this, Elpênor,
how could you journey to the western gloom
swifter afoot than I in the black lugger?"

Elpenor then explains the circumstances of his death and pleads for a decent burial, what we might call the earliest memorial to an unknown sailor:

[9] All quotations from the *Odyssey* are in Robert Fitzgerald's translation (Garden City, N.Y., 1961).

"When you make sail
and put these lodgings of dim Death behind,
you will moor ship, I know, upon Aiaia Island;
there, O my lord, remember me, I pray,
do not abandon me unwept, unburied,
to tempt the gods' wrath, while you sail for home:
but fire my corpse, and all the gear I had,
and build a cairn for me above the breakers—
an unknown sailor's mark for men to come.
Heap up the mound there, and implant upon it
the oar I pulled in life with my companions."

Odysseus promises this "unhappy spirit" the rite he pleads for, and, upon his return to the Island of Aiaia in Book XII, he fulfils his promise devotedly, "weeping while the flame burnt through / corse and equipment."

Seferis draws on this sparse material to create a character who is as representative of contemporary attitudes as Odysseus himself; in fact, the particular role he assigns to Elpenor would indicate that he finds the sensibility of this Homeric figure the one most appropriate to our age. Elpenor appears on a number of occasions in Seferis's verse, but his role is most fully realized in the "Argonaut" section of *Mythistorima* (No. 4) and in the middle section of the poet's most ambitious work, *"Thrush."* In the former of these, Seferis takes up certain motifs suggested by Homer's Elpenor and enlarges them into a portrait of pervasive mediocrity. Elpenor's lack of valor and intelligence become a characteristic submissiveness and insensitivity in the contemporary world, here symbolized by the futile voyage of a crew of modern Argonauts:

And if the soul
is to know itself
it must look
into a soul:
the stranger and enemy, we've seen him in the mirror.

They were fine, my companions, they never complained
about the work or the thirst or the frost,
they had the bearing of trees and waves
that accept the wind and the rain
accept the night and the sun
without changing in the midst of change.
They were fine, whole days
they sweated at the oars with lowered eyes
breathing in rhythm
and their blood reddened a submissive skin.
Sometimes they sang, with lowered eyes
as we were passing the dry island with the barbary figs
to the west, beyond the cape
of the barking dogs.
If it is to know itself, they said
it must look into a soul, they said
and the oars struck the sea's gold
in the sunset.
We went past many capes many islands the sea
leading to another sea, gulls and seals.
Sometimes unfortunate women wept
lamenting their lost children
and others raging sought Alexander the Great
and glories buried in the heart of Asia.
We moored on shores full of night-scents
with birds singing, waters that left on the hands
the memory of great happiness.
But the voyages did not end.
Their souls became one with the oars and the oarlocks
with the solemn face of the prow
with the wake left by the rudder
with the water that shattered their image.
The companions died one by one,
with lowered eyes. Their oars
mark the place where they sleep by the shore.

No one remembers them. Justice.

The "companions" described here project the mediocrity of the present against the nobility of the past, a nobility implicit in the allusion of the Argonauts; come to life in a contemporary world, they are submissive, spineless, unchanging, hollow, Elpenors one and all, while the original Argonauts were heroic to the point of apotheosis. To quote the poet again, "the typical characters have changed in keeping with the passing of time and the different conditions of our world." Their change is further emphasized by the allusion to Alexander the Great and "glories buried in the heart of Asia," glories far in the past and therefore irretrievable, but sought for nevertheless by these wasted souls on a voyage that has no end. Elpenor appears overtly in the concluding lines as we see each of the dead companions sharing the memorial he pleaded for: "Their oars / mark the place where they sleep by the shore"; but fortune is still not with Elpenor and his pliable comrades since, even with oars for markers, "No one remembers them." The poet's final word "Justice" implies that their fate is as it should be, for what have they done to earn a reward reserved for heroes?

In the middle section of "*Thrush*," a long three-part poem that crowned Seferis's experience of World War II, the poet actually brings Elpenor on stage to act out a scene full of significant overtones. It is here that Elpenor assumes his place as a principal in Seferis's mythological drama, and his moment on stage reveals the poet's "mythical method" at its subtlest.[10] The modern setting of this poem is a house by the sea on the island of Poros, the persona's counterpart to Circe's Aiaia. Our modern Odysseus has returned to this house at the conclusion of World War II, and it is full of memories for him, full of images that recall things as they were before wartime disasters turned the world into "an endless hotel." Among the images that his memory resurrects in the opening section of the poem are those of Elpenor and Circe, the former dressed

[10] Seferis's relation to the "mythical method" is discussed more fully in the essay that follows this one.

aptly in white and black (it is his sad fate to be neither extreme), with the Cavafian embellishment of "many-colored jewels," and the latter with "eyelashes quivering, slim-waisted," returning from harbors appropriately hot and sensual. The drama really begins in the second section of the poem when the poet has this man of small valor and limited intellect, this man of merely partial sensibility, approach Circe with seduction in mind—the Circe that no man, including Odysseus, could master without a god's help. The persona introduces the scene that takes place under his window as he would any encounter of its kind in a Greek island town. Again, the setting is real, actual, contemporary; again, the anachronism of the action is what makes the mythical figures totally alive, totally relevant:

SENSUAL ELPENOR

I saw him yesterday standing by the door
below my window; it was about
seven o'clock; there was a woman with him.
He had the look of Elpenor just before he fell
and smashed himself, yet he wasn't drunk.
He was speaking fast, and she
was gazing absently toward the gramophones;
now and then she cut him short to say a word
and then would glance impatiently
toward where they were frying fish: like a cat.
He muttered with a cigarette butt between his lips. . . .

This fast-talking Elpenor, dead butt-end dangling from his lips, older but not much wiser than his Homeric prototype, hasn't got a chance: in the dialogue that follows he attempts to lead up to his "overwhelming question" through metaphors, metaphors that reveal his sensual preoccupations without allowing him to come to the point directly. As the poet himself tells us in his "A Letter on 'Thrush,' " (p. 502), Elpenor seems unable to forget the lasciviousness he experienced when converted into a pig, yet he is incapable of approaching Circe on the subject of carnal love without "comparisons and indirections." Circe, for her part, "like every indifferent woman, has no understanding for this lover; her instincts look elsewhere: at Odysseus." The conversation between these two mythic protagonists beautifully dramatizes the necessary failure in communication between the sentimental sensualist and the sensual realist: Elpenor offers hedonistic images (drawn largely from Seferis's early poetry) and Circe answers him with curt, unimaginative facts. The two cannot possibly get together.

—"Listen. There's this too. In the moonlight
the statues sometimes bend like reeds
in the midst of ripe fruit—the statues;
and the flame becomes a cool oleander,
the flame that burns you, I mean."

—"It's just the light . . . shadows of the night."

—"Maybe the night that split open, a blue pomegranate,
a dark breast, and filled you with stars,
cleaving time.
                    And yet the statues
bend sometimes, dividing desire in two,
like a peach; and the flame
becomes a kiss on the limbs, a sobbing,
and then a cool leaf carried off by the wind;
they bend; they become light with a human weight.
You don't forget it."

                    —"The statues are in the museum."

Seferis says in his essay (p. 503) that Elpenor might have had more success had he used the direct approach of Cavafy—for example: "In the moonlight, the sensual bodies . . ."—rather than the "hybrid escape of the statues." He goes on to say that at Circe's first reply, "Elpenor feels humiliated, reacts,

puts his foot in it even more; his subsequent words are no
longer an invitation to love, but the gaze of a worm looking
out from the fruit of sensual pleasure." This is true of his
second reply, but his third reply suggests a more complex
attitude: though Elpenor may not be completely aware of what
he is saying, his subsequent words offer the first signs of self-
recognition, a sense of what his life might have been had he
not been turned into a pig. We find in him some of that
nostalgia for lost innocence, some of that aspiration to return
to a lost paradise, that make him a legitimate, even sympa-
thetic, companion to the poem's persona:

—"No, they pursue you, why can't you see it?
I mean with their broken limbs,
with their shape from another time, a shape you don't recognize
yet know.
                    It's as though
in the last days of your youth you loved
a woman who was still beautiful, and you were constantly
        afraid,
as you held her naked at noon,
of the memory aroused by your embrace;
were afraid the kiss might betray you
to other beds now of the past
which nevertheless could haunt you
so easily, so easily, and bring to life
images in the mirror, bodies once alive:
their sensuality.
                    It's as though
returning home from some foreign country you happen to open
an old trunk that's been locked up a long time
and find the tatters of clothes you used to wear
on happy occasions, at festivals with many-colored lights,
mirrored, now becoming dim,
and all that remains is the perfume of the absence
of a young form.

Really, those statues are not
the fragments. You yourself are the relic;
they haunt you with a strange virginity
at home, at the office, at receptions for the celebrated,
in the unconfessed terror of sleep;
they speak of things you wish didn't exist
or would happen years after your death,
and that's difficult because . . ."

—"The statues are in the museum.
Good night."

—". . . because the statues are no longer
fragments. We are. The statues bend lightly . . .
Good night."

The "shape from another time" that pursues Elpenor in his
fragmented, inarticulate state, the memory of beautiful mo-
ments, the image of bodies once alive, the strange virginity of
the statues, all speak of a different order of life from what
Elpenor now knows, a life that was once his but that he seems
to recognize having irrevocably lost. There is a degree of pa-
thos in this implicit recognition. His final words to Circe are
not simply those of "*l'homme moyen sensuel*" ambitious be-
yond his means, but the words of a man struggling to escape
the tyranny of memory even while seeming to realize that
memory is the whole substance left to him—as Homer's El-
penor also realized. Though doomed by his own nostalgia—
doomed at least to fail with a realist like Circe—Elpenor here
solicits some of the sympathy for his condition that Homer's
Odysseus felt for the condition of his unburied and unwept
Elpenor. The fact that Seferis's protagonist has no hope of
recovering from his ill fortune through ritual burial makes
him all the more pathetic; it also makes him representative of
a general contemporary condition: that of all men "who seek
expression" without the mind or heart for it and without the
traditional forms that could raise them above their individual

predicament.[11] Elpenor is condemned to a death-in-life without memorial; his only resource is a petrified, fragmented nostalgia for a past irrevocably lost.

The ambivalence in the poet's attitude toward Elpenor—the play of irony against sympathy—is fully intentional: it dramatizes the poet's view that, if this man of no fortune is to be pitied for his condition, the condition nevertheless has its dangers. Seferis remarks in his commentary (pp. 502-503):

> Perhaps you will ask why I write about them [Elpenor and his companions] with sympathy. Because the men who belong to this category, among the heroes (in the Homeric sense, not, for God's sake, in the Carlylian) are the most sympathetic. Even the Homeric Odysseus, when he sees Elpenor, first among the dead, pities him and sheds tears. I do not say lovable or admirable, I say sympathetic, sentimental, mediocre, wasted. ... He [Elpenor] symbolizes those to whom we refer in daily conversation with the expression: "the poor devil." However, let us not forget that these guileless men, exactly because they are "easy," are often the best carriers of an evil which has its source elsewhere.

The "evil" that the poet has in mind reveals itself in the remainder of the poem, but only by implication; one might summarize it as "injustice" in a very Greek sense of the term: all excess that violates the just order of things. Justice in this sense is a matter of balance, of maintaining the equilibrium ordained by the gods. In his commentary the poet alludes to Heraclitus's statement that even the sun cannot pass beyond its proper limits without rousing the Furies that serve Justice. Hubris is a form of injustice; so is the "soul-mongering" of

[11] These themes suggest another link between Seferis and Cavafy, who was much on the poet's mind at the time the poem was composed on postwar Poros, as is suggested by his allusion to Cavafy above and confirmed by his journal of this period (see below, Sef. 3, n. 2). For the role of memory as it is related to sensual nostalgia and ritual in Cavafy's work, see *Cavafy's Alexandria*, pp. 64-67 and 137-138.

war that appears in the poem after Elpenor has left the stage; so is Elpenor's obsessive hedonism. The protagonist's nostalgia has two faces: it is not merely for innocence, youth, vitality, and the like, but also for the animal sensuality, the bestial excesses, of his metamorphosis into a pig. His uncontrolled hedonism finally kills him in Homer: "ignoble death I drank with so much wine"; and, in both Homer and Seferis's poem, his death prohibits his sharing the "liberation" that Odysseus experiences after his visit to the land of the dead—a liberation, the poet tells us, "that some call a return to a lost paradise and others call union with God." Elpenor represents those weak companions who earn their own undoing, despite Tiresias's warning, by hungrily devouring the Oxen of the Sun; this hedonistic violation of the just order of things literally precludes their return to a lost paradise.[12] The implication is that no man can aspire to spiritual liberation until he learns to control his animal appetites, the beast in him that Homer's Circe exploited so cruelly. "The whole question," Seferis says in his commentary, "is how one can honor the Oxen of the Sun, how one can honor the light of every day that God gives one" (p. 505).

To devour the Oxen of the Sun is death; to learn to honor them is the way to liberation. It is Elpenor's fortune to die even before he has a chance to treat his appetite to this most fatal of all meals, but treat he would have. Circe knows him for what he is in Seferis's poem and turns her back on him with a curt "good night." The poet is more generous: he allows Elpenor to speak his own epitaph at the opening of the third section of the poem, when the persona begins his visit to the land of the dead. As in Homer, Elpenor is the first shade to come forward; he makes a gesture in keeping with the poet's "sympathetic" view of him:

"This wood that cooled my forehead

[12] A theme that appears in Seferis's first volume, *Turning Point* (1931), in the poem "The Companions in Hades."

at times when noon burned my veins
will flower in other hands. Take it, I'm giving it to you;
Look, it's wood from a lemon tree . . ."

Sentimental, mediocre, wasted certainly; but the gesture sug-
gests another justification for the degree of pity that both
Homer and Seferis solicit for him. His fortune—represented
by the lemon wood that will flower in other hands—is, after
all, the fortune of most men in his time and ours, and Elpenor
seems to have the virtue (perhaps unlike most men in his time
and ours) of knowing how wasted he is.

Seferis and

the "Mythical Method"

All comparatists recognize the limitations of learning a foreign tradition by way of translation alone; it is part of their mission to break through these limitations and to establish direct access to the foreign literatures that interest them by approaching these literatures in the original. Yet the inaccessibility of modern Greek—the fact that it is taught in so few universities in the United States[1]—normally precludes this kind of direct access even for the committed comparatist; and those readers of poetry without such a commitment who have nevertheless begun to recognize that an exciting tradition lies concealed beyond a language barrier still more or less impenetrable have had to depend entirely on translated texts and on English-speaking editors or reviewers who are themselves too dependent on translated texts. The consequent distortion has sometimes been acute: Cavafy, Sikelianos, and

[1] Though this remark was made in 1968, when the present essay was first delivered as a paper at the University of Maryland symposium on modern Greek literature in the spring of that year, it still holds today, despite some growth in university programs in modern Greek language and literature, e.g., those at Harvard, Princeton, the University of Minnesota, Ohio State University, the University of Florida (Gainesville), Queens College, Wayne State University, and the University of Utah. A complete list of current offerings in modern Greek at the university level is under preparation through the auspices of the Modern Greek Studies Association, which was founded at the Maryland symposium in 1968.

Kazantzakis are to the point here, but perhaps George Seferis most of all, because he seems to have been particularly vulnerable to the prejudices of his English-speaking interpreters, who have found much of his work so close in persuasion and method to the poetry they most admire in their own tradition that they have tended to slight the more indigenous—and sometimes the more original—elements in his work. It will be among my purposes here to review these prejudices (or what some might call natural preferences) and the distortions they have occasioned, in the hope that an assessment of Seferis's work less restricted than the one which prevails in the English-speaking world may emerge. Since I have been among those subject to the prejudices I have in mind, this effort will be something of a self-examination, a review of my own past distortions, compelled by the several years of renewed intimacy with the original text of Seferis's work that the collected English edition of his poetry required.[2]

The first thing that one becomes conscious of on rereading the full Seferis corpus in the original is the number of unfamiliar yet startling poems hidden away in this or that volume, especially from *Book of Exercises* through *Logbook III*. Of course Seferis hasn't done the hiding, and the poems in question seem unfamiliar only because they do not appear in the various selections of Seferis's verse in English translation, including the Keeley-Sherrard selection in *Six Poets of Modern Greece*.[3] One gets the impression, in fact, that there has been

[2] The edition referred to here is that of 1967 (Princeton University Press and Jonathan Cape). The edition was supplemented in 1969 and both revised and extended in 1982, under the new title *George Seferis: Collected Poems*.

[3] This autholony is now out of print. A related anthology of five of the poets, with a revision of the Seferis selection, has now been issued by Denise Harvey Inc. (Athens, 1981) under the title *The Dark Crystal*, and by Princeton University Press (1981) under the title *Voices of Modern Greece*. Other relevant selections are *The King of Asine and Other Poems*, trans. Bernard Spencer, Nanos Valaoritis, and Lawrence Durrell (London, 1948), *Poems*, trans. Rex Warner (London and Boston, 1961), and the Seferis selection in *Modern Greek Poetry*, trans. Kimon Friar (New York, 1973).

some kind of conspiracy on the part of Seferis's English-speaking editors to keep out those poems that do not quite fit the classicist, the mythic, or the Eliotesque patterns that made Seferis's work immediately appealing when it first appeared in England in 1948: forgotten poems like "Piazza San Nicolo" and "Narration" and "Les anges sont blancs," to cite examples from a single volume, *Logbook I*, which now strikes me as Seferis's most rewarding after *Mythistorima*.[4] I will turn later in this essay to my reasons for thinking it so; my point here is that the English reader of Seferis's poetry would have small basis for making a judgment one way or the other, because the three selections from this volume that have been available to him[5] include, together, less than half of the poems in the volume; and if these particular selections are a bit too varied and apparently casual to indicate a conspiracy, they do suggest to me a shared preference which bears further investigation. The three poems mentioned are all poems that seem to translate an intensely felt personal experience into general symbols that have no evident classical, postclassical, or neoclassical antecedents, and the best of the three, "Narration," gives the reader no firm grip on even a personal antecedent: the symbol stands on its own terms entirely, undecorated by literary, mythic, or even geographic allusion, unmodified by any implicit or explicit comment within the poem, yet fashioned with the kind of precision that makes its meaning both dramatic and subtle:[6]

[4] This 1968 opinion presumably did not view Seferis's very rewarding poem "*Thrush*" as the equivalent of a volume, and the opinion was offered before there had been time for a proper digestion on my part of *Three Secret Poems*, which first appeared in Greek in December, 1966. I would now qualify the opinion by suggesting that it was the product of enthusiasm generated by a renewed discovery of several forgotten poems in Seferis and should not be taken to diminish much fine poetry that appeared after *Logbook I*.

[5] In 1968 (see n. 3 above).

[6] There is one comment outside the poem that establishes a certain mythic genealogy for the central figure in the poem: Seferis tells us in his "A Letter on 'Thrush' " (p. 502) that "the 'man who walks along weeping' is a *grotesco* sketch of Elpenor; indeed, he is perhaps the most kin to [the Elpenor] of 'Thrush.' " For further context in English, see the translation of the full text

That man walks along weeping
no one can say why
sometimes they think he's weeping for lost loves
like those that torture us so much
on summer beaches with the gramophones.

Other people go about their business
endless paper, children growing up, women
ageing awkwardly.
He has two eyes like poppies
like cut spring poppies
and two trickles in the corners of his eyes.

He walks along the streets, never lies down
striding small squares on the earth's back
instrument of a boundless pain
that's finally lost all significance.

Some have heard him speak
to himself as he passed by
about mirrors broken years ago
about broken forms in the mirrors
that no one can ever put together again.
Others have heard him talk about sleep
images of horror on the threshold of sleep
faces unbearable in their tenderness.

We've grown used to him, he's presentable and quiet
only that he walks along weeping continually
like willows on a riverbank you see from the train
as you wake uncomfortably some clouded dawn.

We've grown used to him; like everything else you're
        used to
he doesn't stand for anything
and I talk to you about him because I can't find
anything that you're not used to;
I pay my respects.

of the letter by James Stone in *Journal of the Hellenic Diaspora*, Vol. 7, No. 2 (Summer, 1980).

What distinguishes this poem first of all is the character of the governing symbol: this mysterious man who walks the streets weeping continually. The clues to what he is weeping about build up through the poem—from the lost loves mentioned in the opening lines, to the broken forms in the mirrors, to those images of horror on the threshold of sleep—until it seems he has taken upon himself the burden of the world's past sorrows or, if not the world's, at least that "kaimos tis Romiosinis" which best characterizes the Greek experience in Seferis's view.[7] Yet as the poet projects these clues to the symbol's meaning, he also tells us that the man is the "instrument of a boundless pain that's finally lost all significance," and the irony of this circumstance—of a clearly significant sorrow that's lost all significance—also builds up through the poem until the surprise ending, when the poet turns, with a subtle shift in the pronoun, from a casual generality to a specific confrontation with the reader:

We've grown used to him; like everything else you're used to
he doesn't stand for anything
and I talk to you about him because I can't find
anything that you're not used to;
I pay my respects.

We now see that the weeping man's boundless pain has lost all significance because of our having complacently grown used to him. This loaded symbol of our sorrow has been emptied of its meaning by our casually taking it for granted, so that it ends up meaning for us; but just in case the reader complacently relaxes with his understanding of this irony, the poet turns to him in the last three lines to remind him of just how much he too has come to take for granted, not only the sorrow the weeping man represents, but everything else as well. It is hard to think of a more dramatic instance of a poet's

[7] The phrase "kaimos tis Romiosinis," which Seferis has always regarded as untranslatable, roughly means "the sorrowful yearning of modern Greece."

bringing the reader directly into the action of a poem since Eliot's use of the Baudelaire line: "You! hypocrite lecteur!—mon semblable,—mon frère!" at the end of Section I of *The Waste Land*. But Seferis's mode is less literary and therefore more moving, especially when we remember that the poem was written during those all-too-complacent months preceding the outbreak of World War II. Our man of sorrows and our attitude toward him thus become metaphoric revelations of a specific tragic moment in time, in contemporary history: this is the kind of actuality that always lies behind Seferis's most effective symbols.

How could a poem as fine as this escape the notice of all of Seferis's English translators? Perhaps, one suspects, because it is not the kind of poem they were looking for to bring Seferis to a world whose image of Greece still depends so heavily on classical and neoclassical sources.[8] The poem they were looking for is the last one in the same volume, "The King of Asine"—the one which became the title poem of the first selection of Seferis's work in English. "The King of Asine" is also a poem at least partly about a "contemporary sorrow," but it treats this subject in a way perhaps more accessible to the Anglo-Saxon literary sensibility that has been nurtured on the work of Eliot and Pound: the poem has an epigraph from Homer, an elaborated mythic context, a poet-persona controlling the tone and the argument, and so forth. This is not to deny that it is a brilliant poem in its own way, as I hope to demonstrate below; it is merely to suggest that it is a somewhat different kind of poem from "Narration" and a group of related poems in *Logbook I*, each of which transforms a personal experience or recognition into a metaphor that precisely defines the character of a contemporary attitude, each of which dramatizes the mood of the times, no matter how elusive or complex, in a relatively direct manner, with few of the literary aids that we find in Seferis's Anglo-American sources.

[8] A theme that is explored further below in "Elytis and the Greek Tradition."

I have in mind poems such as "Piazza San Nicolo," "Our Sun," "The Return of the Exile," "Interlude of Joy," "The Last Day," "Morning," and "Les anges sont blancs." These are the poems that really set the tone of *Logbook I*, that serve to distinguish this volume from the others before and immediately after it, that perhaps project a more original image of Seferis's work than that with which his English readers are most familiar. But what finally leads me to believe that this volume must be regarded as Seferis's best—certainly his best before *Logbook III*—is the new way he chooses to handle what I have called his "mythical method": the method of *Mythistorima* and of most poems known to his English-speaking readers.

When I offered the phrase "mythical method" in connection with Seferis's *Mythistorima* some twelve years ago in an article on Eliot and Seferis,[9] I was still too close to a dissertation I had written on English influences in the poetry of Cavafy and Seferis—still too enamored with the possibility of establishing parallels, borrowings, and other comparative interests—to look at this aspect of the poet's work with full objectivity. I found myself seduced by my comparative theme into seeing Seferis's method almost entirely in the terms that Eliot had used in his famous 1923 review of Joyce's *Ulysses*, where the phrase "mythical method" first appears.[10] I said in the article that in *Mythistorima* Seferis attempts, in Eliot's words, to give a "shape and a significance to the immense panorama of futility and anarchy which is contemporary history" by using the mythology of Homer to manipulate "a continuous parallel between contemporaneity and antiquity." This is of course general enough to be unexceptionable.[11] But then I went on to say: "Seferis's method is that of *The Waste Land*. . . . What Eliot attempts with the Fisher King, the Phoenician Sailor, and

[9] *Comparative Literature* 8 (Summer, 1956), pp. 214-226.

[10] *The Dial* (November, 1923), p. 483; reprinted in *Selected Prose of T. S. Eliot*, ed. Frank Kermode (New York, 1975), pp. 175-178.

[11] The recent exception taken to it by Nasos Vayenas is discussed in the Addendum to this essay.

Ferdinand Prince of Naples, Seferis attempts with Ulysses, Elpenor, and Orestes," and I concluded that since the synthesis of past and present through the agency of myth becomes the central preoccupation of Seferis's art for the first time in *Mythistorima*, "a preoccupation that remains more or less constant throughout his subsequent work," we could reasonably assume that his discovery of Eliot's poetry a few years before the publication of *Mythistorima* encouraged the development of this method.

There are several aspects of my argument in the 1956 article that call for reappraisal. To begin with, is Seferis's method really that of *The Waste Land* in any but the broadest terms? Does he even handle his mythological characters in the same manner? Finally, is it really accurate to say that his preoccupation with the "mythical method" remains more or less constant throughout his subsequent work? It seems to me now that each of these conclusions emerged from an oversimplified view of Seferis's work and of his affinity to Eliot; each requires further qualification and elaboration if a more precise estimate of Seferis's use of mythological sources is to be suggested, along with a more just estimate of his originality.

The reappraisal should begin with *Mythistorima*, a crucial poem both in Seferis's own development and in the study of his relation to Eliot. It seems to me that there is a fundamental difference in method between this poem and *The Waste Land*, the work by Eliot that most critics consider Seferis's first English source, especially since Seferis completed a full translation of *The Waste Land* in 1936, the year after *Mythistorima* was published. Eliot's method in *The Waste Land* is that of poetic collage: an arrangement of fragments that vary in rhythm, tone, style, and mood, with only a few connecting links in theme and structure to tie the fragments together into a relatively coherent whole. Admittedly, one of the unifying devices is a recurrent mythology, but even this is fragmented, drawn from a variety of traditions: Egyptian, Greek, Biblical, Oriental, Anglo-Saxon, and Wagnerian, to name the most obvious. And there is no unifying "voice," no dominant persona, in the poem. Though Eliot identifies Tiresias, in a note, as "the most important personage in the poem, uniting all the rest," he also admits that Tiresias is a "mere spectator and not indeed a 'character' "; Tiresias sees all but speaks rarely, and when he does speak, his voice is only one among many others of differing styles, including those of other "prophetic" personages such as the Fisher King and Ezekiel. In contrast to this highly eclectic mode, Seferis chooses in *Mythistorima* to use a single mythology, a single voice, a single tone, and a single style. His method is not collage but a kind of chiaroscuro: an arrangement of light and dark parts so as to reveal a unifying sensibility that grows directly out of his myth and that speaks with the continuity, the single-mindedness, of a character in fiction.

The poet himself gives us the terms most relevant to his mode in his note on the title: "MYTHISTORIMA—it is its two components that made me choose the title of this work: MYTHOS, because I have used, clearly enough, a certain mythology; ISTORIA [both "story" and "history"], because I have tried to express, with some coherence, circumstances that are as independent from myself as the characters in a novel." The "circumstances" that the poet has in mind are carefully ordered by the poem's persona, and this persona, given substance by both a consistent style and a unified mythology, assumes the dramatic function of a central character who is involved in the action of each of the twenty-four sections of the poem and who speaks—as the poet indicates—for a larger sensibility than the poet's own. His characteristic stance, at some point in almost every one of the twenty-four sections, is that of spokesman for a first person plural, a "we" that stands first of all for a group of contemporary voyagers with direct Homeric antecedents but that gathers resonance as we move through the poem until it seems to represent something more than simply a modern Odysseus and his lost companions, something more than a nostalgic exile leading his foolish Elpenor and crew toward those beautiful islands just out of reach: it ends up symbolizing the latest manifestation of the

Greek spirit, of that "kaimos tis Romiosinis" which was mentioned earlier as central to Seferis's vision. It is a "we" in which the contemporary Greek reader is meant to share as no Anglo-Saxon can quite share in the experience of a Fisher King, or of a Ferdinand Prince of Naples, or even of that androgynous, collective Tiresias, all of whom are so foreign to our world that we cannot really tell who is appearing before us exactly when in the poem without Eliot's extensive program notes. The advantage of Seferis's method is immediacy: no one need wonder whose voice tells us "in the summers we were lost in the agony of days that couldn't die," or "only the grooves on the well's lip / remind us of our past happiness," or "Among these decimated villages on this promontory, open to the south wind / with the mountain range in front of us hiding you, / who will calculate for us the cost of our decision to forget?" or "we knew that the islands were beautiful / somewhere round about here where we are groping— / a little lower or a little higher, / the slightest distance," or "Our country is closed in, all mountains / that day and night have the low sky as their roof. / We have no rivers, we have no wells, we have no springs, / only a few cisterns—and these empty—that echo, and that we worship." It is always the same tragic tone of voice in *Mythistorima*, even when it speaks in the first person as lover or exile, and even when it momentarily takes on the mask of Orestes or Jason rather than of Odysseus; and it always speaks in symbols that belong to the history and landscape of Greece, symbols rendered in that consistently unadorned, chiaroscuro style—the dark tones relieved occasionally by bright islands, almond trees blossoming, and many-colored, glittering ships—which gives the poem's voice its unique character.

I would still conclude that Seferis found a kindred spirit in Eliot during the period that he was working on *Mythistorima*, and I would still suggest that the element which Seferis himself tells us most appealed to him in *The Waste Land*—the "dramatic manner of expression," the treatment of "thirsting despair" through actual human character and "the elements of tragedy"[12]—very likely inspired the Greek poet to move from the rather vague symbolizing of *The Cistern* to the more tragic voice and much more dramatic mode of expression in *Mythistorima*; but the mode is nevertheless very much Seferis's own, and if it can be related to Eliot's (as well as to Joyce's and Yeats's) in the broadest sense,[13] it is hardly accurate to call it one and the same. Nor does Seferis's mode remain more or less constant, as my early view would have it: neither in terms of preoccupation nor of method. This too calls for further reappraisal. I have already suggested that the characteristic mode of *Logbook I* is not rooted in a transformed mythology—a resurrection and metamorphosis of mythic characters to serve as symbols of a contemporary condition—but in a universalizing of deeply felt personal experience or insight, with little aid from analogies of any kind. Fewer than a third of the poems in *Logbook I* make use of a specific mythology, and in several the use is confined to allusions.[14] Only one poem out of eleven in *Logbook II*, the poem "Stratis the Mariner Among the Agapanthi," depends on an extended mythic analogue to a contemporary theme. It is true that the long poem *"Thrush,"* published in 1947, marks a return to some of the mythological preoccupations that we find in *Mythistorima*, and it is also true that many of the poems in *Logbook III* make use of legendary or historical sources,[15] but the method of these later works bears only a tenuous relation to that of *Mythistorima*—so tenuous that to use the term "constancy" in this connection is to be misleading.

This review of Seferis's later work implies an "inconstancy" in his mythical method. It is the inconstancy of progress, of a developing artistry in his handling of parallels between contemporaneity and antiquity. I have suggested elsewhere that one of the distinguishing characteristics of Seferis's method

---

[12] See "Letter to a Foreign Friend," *On the Greek Style*, pp. 167-168.

[13] As is illustrated more fully in the Addendum below.

[14] As in "The Last Day"; see Sef. 3 below.

[15] Some of these sources are identified in the discussion of "Helen" and "Salamis in Cyprus" in Sef. 3.

in *Mythistorima* is that he usually offers an appropriate set-
ting—a poetically realistic setting—when he has legendary
figures appear on his stage; as he "attempts to carry the reader
to the level of myth, the level of timeless universalities, he
wins his sympathy and belief by convincingly representing the
present reality sustaining his myth—a contemporary, Greek
reality always."[16] A number of examples of this technique
could be cited from *Mythistorima* and poems of that period;
I offered No. 12, which opens with a description of a solitary
chapel and a whitewashed hut among a few burnt pines and
then surprisingly brings Odysseus and his companions on stage,
against this contemporary backdrop, to mend their broken
oars, as though anachronistic survivors of a grounded cruise
ship. No. 9 will do just as well:

> The harbor is old, I can't wait any longer
> for the friend who left for the island of pine trees
> or the friend who left for the island of plane trees
> or the friend who left for the open sea.
>
> I stroke the rusted cannons, I stroke the oars
> so that my body may revive and decide.
> The sails give off only the smell
> of salt from the other storm.
>
> If I chose to remain alone, what I longed for
> was solitude, not this kind of waiting,
> my soul shattered on the horizon,
> these lines, these colors, this silence.
>
> The night's stars take me back to the anticipation
> of Odysseus waiting for the dead among the asphodels.
> When we moored here among the asphodels we hoped
>   to find
> the gorge that saw Adonis wounded.

[16] Above, pp. 53-54. For a further comment by the poet on the relation
between the particular and the mythical or universal in his use of landscape,
see below, "Postscript: A Conversation with Seferis."

The poem opens with what can be taken for an entirely contemporary state of mind: among the lines, colors, and rusted cannons of a modern harbor, the persona finds himself isolated, his friends gone off to other islands, and the solitude he hoped for turned to a kind of paralysis that prohibits decision and action. But suddenly, in the last stanza, his nervous waiting for release of some kind becomes an anticipation, an expectation of the deliverance that Odysseus knew while waiting to consult the dead about his voyage home. Again with a striking anachronism, our contemporary traveler actually becomes part of a new Homeric action: the "I" shifts abruptly to "we," a "we" that no longer speaks simply as the traveler and his island-hopping friends but also as Odysseus and his weak companions, who have come up as ghostly analogues to moor their black galley near a meadow of asphodel, reminiscent of the country of the dead. The poem concludes with a brilliant touch: the resurrected Odysseus seems as lost in our world as is our modern traveler, because in the context of this poem, what he has found is not quite what he was looking for; what he was looking for was not this meadow of asphodel before him, but the gorge that saw Adonis wounded. In both Nos. 12 and 9, the anachronism is at the heart of the poet's intention, and it works in two ways: the contemporary traveler on the lookout for a lost island paradise participates in Odysseus's fate, and the universal aspect of Odysseus's fate is given a new twist by his coming to life in those modern "circumstances"—circumstances of the loss of direction and purpose, the loss of expression, and finally, the loss of a substantial relation to the past—that constitute the recurring themes of *Mythistorima*.

So much for the method of Seferis's middle period; in what way does his elaboration of this method in later poems suggest not constancy but progress? I have so far emphasized that Seferis always begins with a dramatization of some concrete reality in the present and then moves from this to the more universal, mythic implications of his reality. It is a method clearly related to that of Eliot and Joyce, but Seferis has the advantage of dealing with a present that immediately evokes the past he wishes to resurrect: his characters, settings, even his language can raise mythic overtones without the slightest strain because reality and myth exist in natural conjunction, as is not always the case in the mythic landscapes of Eliot's London and of Joyce's Dublin. But Seferis did not fully exploit his advantage in *Mythistorima*. The landscape of that poem, the concrete reality at the root of his myth, though always Greek in its details, remains nevertheless a more generalized landscape than most he later chose to use. When the sea merges to the westward with a mountain range in No. 7, we do not know which sea in particular nor which range; nor do we know what specific harbors our souls approach on the rotten brine-soaked timbers of No. 8, any more than we recognize the harbor of No. 9 as one that suggests a particular name; and the rocks, burnt pines, and solitary chapel of No. 12, or the empty cisterns and wells of Nos. 10 and 15, could be found anywhere in Greece. There is, of course, a point to this degree of vagueness: it permits the poet to assert immediately the symbolic values of his landscape, those that convey throughout the poem his own image of thirsting despair; but it also has the danger of all immediately symbolic landscapes: the reader may feel on occasion that he has already covered some of the same territory in another poet's imaginative world— for example, in the concluding section of *The Waste Land*, where we also find "mountains of rock without water" and "voices singing out of empty cisterns and exhausted wells" and an empty chapel in a "decayed hole among the mountains." Contrast the relatively generalized landscape of *Mythistorima* with this, from "The King of Asine," in *Logbook I.*

All morning long we looked around the citadel
starting from the shaded side, there where the sea,
green and without luster—breast of a slain peacock—
received us like time without an opening in it.
Veins of rock dropped down from high above,

twisted vines, naked, many-branched, coming alive
at the water's touch, while the eye following them
struggled to escape the tiresome rocking,
losing strength continually.

On the sunny side a long empty beach
and the light striking diamonds on the huge walls.
No living thing, the wild doves gone
and the king of Asine, whom we've been trying to find
    for two years now,
unknown, forgotten by all, even by Homer,
only one word in the *Iliad* and that uncertain,
thrown here like the gold burial mask.
You touched it, remember its sound? Hollow in the light
like a dry jar in dug earth:
the same sound that our oars make in the sea.
The king of Asine a void under the mask
everywhere with us everywhere with us, under a name:
"Asinin te . . . Asinin te"

This landscape is first of all particular and literal: a precise
representation of an actual site, as anyone who has seen the
acropolis of Asine—especially as it was at the time the poem
appeared—will immediately recognize. The symbolic and mythic
values of this landscape are not asserted until we are well into
the second stanza: "No living thing, the wild doves gone /
and the king of Asine, whom we've been trying to find for
two years now, / unknown, forgotten by all. . . ." At this point
in the poem, they come in almost unnoticed, as inconspicuous
as symbol and myth ought to be, because the absence of living
things, including even the ghost of the dead king, seems as
much a natural fact of the setting as those veins of rock and
those light-struck walls. The literalness, the particularity, of
this landscape not only precludes any sharing of common
symbols, but it also prepares the reader to accept the literary
allusion to Homer as something more vital than simply an-
other rehearsal of a popular poetic device: this is, after all, the

actual home of the King of Asine; he is not arbitrarily brought into this setting to give it a mythological chic that profundity cannot give it; and Homer's "forgotten phrase, the "Asinin te" that becomes the poem's refrain, merely reinforces the sense of loss, the sense of a heroic site abandoned to "rain, wind, and ruin" that the persona's morning search around the deserted citadel has already suggested to us. The poem's theme of a failed quest for the vital past is thus supported by particularities in a way that the themes of some sections of *Mythistorima* are not, and the poem builds from reality to myth to meaning in both a more original and a more subtle manner.

The best of Seferis's late "mythic" poems exploit this, rather than his earlier, mode. In *"Thrush,"* the literal landscape is the island of Poros—counterpart to Circe's Aiaia—with its mansion "Galini" (Serenity) and the sunken wreck that gives the poem its title; in "Helen" it is Platres and its nightingales; in "Memory II" it is Ephesus; in "Salamis in Cyprus" it is what the title indicates, as is also true of "Engomi." Each of these poems makes use of an identified setting, described in more or less detail to give a particularity to the metaphors, the history, and the mythology that are its central preoccupations, and each is stronger for doing so. "The King of Asine" can thus be seen as another turning point in Seferis's work, not because it was the first of his poems to offer an identified landscape, but because the poet's careful use of his chosen setting to create a literal backdrop for his mythology established a technique that we find in some of the best work of later volumes. And it is this exciting development, added to the contribution of poems like "Narration" and "The Last Day," that leads me to call *Logbook I* the most rewarding of Seferis's volumes before his Cyprus poems.

This being so, why did I suggest earlier that "The King of Asine" may not be the best poem in the volume, as critics have generally taken it to be? My hesitation about it begins when, after the two stanzas quoted above, we are offered a series of images meant to convey the source of the void which

is everywhere with us, the root of the contemporary sorrow
which is supposed to give the poem its urgency:

Behind the large eyes the curved lips the curls
carved in relief on the gold cover of our existence
a dark spot that you see traveling like a fish
in the dawn calm of the sea:
a void everywhere with us.
And the bird that flew away last winter
with a broken wing:
abode of life,
and the young woman who left to play
with the dogteeth of summer
and the soul that sought the lower world squeaking
and the country like a large plane-leaf swept along by the
    torrent of the sun
with the ancient monuments and the contemporary sorrow.

I find the images here—the bird, the young woman, the soul,
the country—though haunting, though rhetorically moving
and persuasive, rather too obscurely modified to convey a
dramatic meaning. Why is the bird with broken wing an "abode
of life?" What does it connote, in sequence, for the young
woman "to play with the dogteeth of summer?" And is it not
something more than "the torrent of the sun" that is sweeping
the country along like a plane-leaf in the years 1938 to 1940
(as the poem is dated), years that had a very precise source
for the contemporary sorrow? I also find the concluding stan-
zas, though beautiful in rhythm and poetic gesture, no less
obscure in defining the character of the void that the poet
reasserts on entering the poem overtly as a speaker to com-
ment on the implications of the landscape that he has set
before us:

And the poet lingers, looking at the stones, and asks himself
does there really exist
among these ruined lines, edges, points, hollows, and curves

does there really exist
here where one meets the path of rain, wind, and ruin
does there exist the movement of the face, shape of the
    tenderness
of those who've shrunk so strangely in our lives,
those who remained the shadow of waves and thoughts with
    the sea's boundlessness
or perhaps no, nothing is left but the weight
the nostalgia for the weight of a living existence
there where we now remain unsubstantial, bending
like the branches of a terrible willow-tree heaped in
    permanent despair
while the yellow current slowly carries down rushes
    uprooted in the mud
image of a form that the sentence to everlasting bitterness
    has turned to stone:
the poet a void.

The quality and source of our "unsubstantial" existence—the heart of the poet's insight about contemporary circumstances—come through to us only metaphorically, in images that remain memorable for their emotional rather than intellectual precision: the terrible willow-tree heaped in permanent despair, the rushes uprooted in the mud, the form turned to stone by the sentence to everlasting bitterness. We end our reading of the poem as the poet himself does: still caught up in a question.

My small reservation about "The King of Asine" may seem less arbitrary if I place it in the context of another poem of the same period, "The Last Day," which seems to me to present related themes less vaguely yet equally effectively, themes having to do with the mood of contemporary sorrow and the search for a "heroic" attitude in a time dominated by indecisiveness, insubstantiality, and the threat of extinction. This poem, dated "Feb. '39," is discussed in some detail in the essay that follows, with specific reference to the poet's experience of World War II, but let me summarize here the ways in which its treatment of related material may be contrasted to that of the relevant stanzas from "The King of Asine" quoted above. The mode of the poem is also to a degree allusive, as I indicate in my more detailed commentary, but the image of "contemporary sorrow" and its attendant themes do not depend so much on rhetorical evocation as either simple assertion "in the manner of G.S." ("Yet each of us earns his death, his own death, which belongs to no one else / and this game is life") or dramatic representation through telling episodes and characters in action ("The soldiers presented arms as it began to drizzle"; the persona's friend and her jarring question: "How are we going to die?"; and the couple at the end going home to turn on the light inside because they are sick of the dusk that the world offers them outside). Much of the poem has just that simplicity and directness which are missing in related sections of "The King of Asine," yet the poem shapes a statement that seems to me no less subtle, no less moving (even capable, apparently, of rousing strong if unexpected political response: see Sef. 3, n. 9).

Admittedly this estimate reflects a rather subjective preference on my part for the narrative and dramatic over the rhetorical mode in Seferis. Yet there is no need for us to choose one or the other poem; both are among Seferis's finest, and the mode of each has virtues that particular readers will respond to in keeping with their individual taste. Whatever the reader's preference, this comparison and others outlined above may suggest that there are a number of poems in Seferis's later volumes which have not, either here or in Greece, received the attention they deserve, and that among these are a few gems, often hidden from Seferis's English-speaking readers, which will surely reward those who take the time to explore the full corpus of his poetry.

ADDENDUM

SOME TEN YEARS after this essay appeared in *Comparative Literature Studies*,[17] Nasos Vayenas offered a rather lengthy

[17] Vol. 6, No. 2 (June, 1969).

commentary on it in his study of Seferis, *The Poet and the Dancer*. This study strikes me as the best book-length exploration of Seferis's work to appear in Greece.[18] It is especially astute in establishing the character of the poet's relation to French literature and to relevant poets in the modern Greek tradition. It also provides an excellent account of the many sources, including those in the poet's own work, that helped to shape Seferis's most complicated late poem, "*Thrush*." Since Vayenas gives much attention to the question of Eliot's relation to Seferis in general, and to my views on the subject in particular—specifically with reference to the "mythical method"—I feel that some response to his commentary is in order if the present essay is to stand for something more than merely an early introduction to the much debated question of Eliot's assumed influence on the Greek poet, especially in connection with the composition of *Mythistorima*.

Vayenas gives careful attention to the background of the relationship between the two poets, particularly to Seferis's development of like concerns and his assimilation of shared sources in the French tradition before he became acquainted with Eliot, and Vayenas explores both similarities and dissimilarities in the theory, practice, and philosophical orientation of the two poets. In the discussion of specific texts, he is less convincing in his presentation of arguments for or against Eliot's influence—except in the case of "*Thrush*," where this aspect of the commentary is both shrewd and helpful—and I find his discussion of the role of myth in the two poets rather pedantic when not actually wrongheaded (one sees the ghostly image of the doctoral dissertation that fathered the book peeping through his text in this section of his study, as it did in my own first essay on Seferis and Eliot). To be precise, I find that Vayenas's argument with reference to *Mythistorima* reveals a misinterpretation both of Eliot's intention in offering the phrase "mythical method" and of Seferis's adaptation of

---

[18] The best book-length study in English is the 1982 Princeton doctoral dissertation of Rachel Hadas, a brilliantly perceptive and comprehensive account of related imagery in Seferis and Frost, to be published by Bucknell University Press.

the method (whether conscious or unconscious). Vayenas claims that the term "mythical method" is not relevant to a number of poems in the *Mythistorima* volume, e.g., Nos. 7, 8, 10, and 15, because in these "there is no mythical intimation—the poems refer only to contemporary reality—and one wonders why Keeley uses them as examples of Seferis's mythical method."[19] And he goes on to say:

> ... most of the poems in the volume do not have any mythological reference and refer exclusively to the contemporary reality. And there is nothing to show that because the mythical method is used in some of its parts, the whole work is "mythical." *Mythistorima* is not a poem written with the mythical method but one that also includes the mythical method. Nor is it, like the poems of Stratis Thalassinos, a work in one voice, but a synthesis with many voices and many masks, which are interchanged in order to express the drama of a composite reality.[20]

I would counter this view by returning to what Eliot actually says when he introduces the term "mythical method" in his review of Joyce's *Ulysses* (in fact, the only instance of its use in Eliot's criticism), and also to what Seferis tells us about his use of myth in *Mythistorima*. Vayenas believes that Eliot's "description [in the review of *Ulysses*] shows that in the mythical method the myth is used as a structual element, as a kind of diagram that helps the poet to express his experience more objectively. In other words, the mythical method is an objective correlative in the form of a mythical story."[21] What Eliot in fact says is that the method—which consists of "manipulating a continuous parallel between contemporaneity and antiquity"—is "simply a way of controlling, of ordering, of giving a shape and a significance to the immense panorama of futility and anarchy which is contemporary history." "Con-

[19] P. 151.
[20] P. 154.
[21] Pp. 151-152.

trolling," "ordering," and "shap[ing]" a "continuous paral-lel" are the key terms; there is nothing here about expressing experience objectively (Vayenas's introduction of the term "objective correlative" from Eliot's 1919 essay on *Hamlet* to help him explain Eliot's description of Joyce's method in *Ulys-ses* seems to me rather arbitrary and misleading, quite aside from the term's having become a cliché of modern criticism that has been applied so broadly and frequently over the years as to have lost much of its usefulness in any but the contexts in which it was first evoked).[22] Eliot concludes his commentary on Joyce by indicating that the mythical method may be seen as a possible substitute for the narrative method, and he again emphasizes that it is a step toward "order and form."

It is in the quite general terms of Eliot's review—the only terms he himself allows—that we must express Seferis's affin-ity to Eliot in connection with the "mythical method." Eliot obviously never intended the phrase to express a critical doc-trine that could define—correctly or incorrectly, in Vayenas's view—the particular technique of individual poems in a se-quence or the individual chapters of a novel (his specific text was of course Joyce's "epic" novel, and Eliot gave some at-tention to what Joyce's new work contributed to expanding our image of the form of the novel). In short, the "mythical method" is not so much a matter of overt or covert, direct or indirect, uses of mythology in individual poems or chapters that evoke a contemporary reality; it is a way of ordering and controlling the progress of related poems (e.g., those in Yeats that draw on Irish mythology, as Eliot himself suggests), or a long poem of many parts such as *The Waste Land*, or a sequence of poems, or a particular kind of modern novel, all

[22] Though Seferis found it useful in commenting on Cavafy's progressive rejection of "the unframed expression of emotion" in his "Cafavy and Eliot—a Comparison" (*On the Greek Style*, pp. 145-146), the same essay in which he maintains, in another context having to do with the use of historical time in the two poets, that the mythical method "is not only adumbrated, but is systematically employed by Cavafy long before the appearance of *Ulysses* and Joyce, and long before Yeats also" (p. 137).

of which are meant to project a *continuous* parallel between past and present, antiquity and contemporaneity. That Seferis intended his sequence of poems called *Mythistorima* to be read with this kind of continuous ordering principle in mind is patently evident from his note on the title of the poem. His phrase "I have used, clearly enough, a certain mythology," and his expressed attempt at "some coherence"—as well as the seqential implications of the title as a whole, which literally means "novel"—suggest not merely the presence of occasional overt mythic allusions in individual poems, allusions of the kind that can be easily catalogued (see Vayenas, *The Poet and the Dancer*, pp. 151 ff.),[23] but a continuous framework, an

[23] This critic's penchant for cataloguing and for establishing what is a "correct" application of the term "mythical method" results in a number of rather pedantic distinctions that finally make it difficult to apply Eliot's very general terms to Seferis's practice at any period. He tells us "what Keeley considers a characteristic indication of the mythical method in *Mythistorima* happens in only two of the poems (Nos. 9, 12), where the ancient myth makes—or we can say that it makes—its appearance. In five other poems (Nos. 3, 4, 16, 17, 20), the opposite happens. The mythical dimension is suggested (or declared) from the beginning, as much by the titles, which constitute evident ancient allusions (Nos. 3, 4, 16, 17, 20), as by, in some others, the description of the opening lines, which conveys an ancient feeling (Nos. 4, 16, 17). In Nos. 7, 8, 10, and 15, there is no mythical intimation. ...." My point regarding Nos. 9 and 12 was originally presented without specific reference to the mythical method in *Mythistorima* but more generally to Seferis's natural and unpretentious exploitation of "the survival of mythic gods and heroes in the landscape of Modern Greece" by "convincingly representing the present reality sustaining his myth—a contemporary, Greek reality always—" when he allows his legendary figures to appear on stage, a view that the poet himself seems to have endorsed (see n. 16 above). In the context of *Mythistorima*, the comment obviously refers first of all to those sections in which mythical figures actually appear on stage and take part in the poem's action to some degree (as in Nos. 9 and 12), but it would be pedantry to exclude the less overt appearance of mythic figures—again following a poetically realistic description of landscape—in the concluding lines of Nos. 7, 8, 10, and 15, as is illustrated below in this Addendum. Yet the debate here becomes rather one-sided, since Vayenas does not see any mythic intimations in these four sections—this despite the "offering" in No. 7, the islands just out of reach in No. 8, the Symplegades and never-ended voyages in No. 10, and the lost companion in No. 15. And we learn later in his

overall structure (not just a "structural element") that can serve to give the twenty-four poems in the sequence the kind of coherence that narrative supplied in the traditional novel, as Eliot suggests in his review.

In the case of Eliot's model for the mythical method, Joyce's new kind of "epic" novel, the presence of the myth, though persistent, is generally covert.[24] In *Mythistorima*, the presence is sometimes overt, sometimes covert, but with or without the benefit of direct allusion, the "certain mythology" is always there to give the poet's image of contemporary reality a particular shape and significance, as it does throughout Joyce's novel. It is not a "method" in the sense of a technique that

---

argument that "with the exception of 'Helen' and '*Thrush*,' the poet does not use the mythical method in any of the poems that Keeley refers to as mature examples of Seferis's mythical method." In "The King of Asine," for example, the

> allusion to the myth is consumed in a correlation of contemporary and ancient fate (there is no 'intimation of Homer' but a named allusion to Homer). This correlation is not an objective correlative but an objective confirmation. The myth is simply useful as one term of a comparison, and the difference between its use here and in *Mythistorima* is the difference between a simile and a metaphor

—this though such a distinction carries us very far from Eliot's description of the mythical method and even farther from the poem itself, which concludes with an image of the poet-persona (using the first person plural) "touching with our fingers his [the ancient King of Asine's] touch upon the stones." And, for a final example, we learn that "in 'Engomi' there is no myth. There is only the spectacle of the excavation of an ancient city and the description of the experience the poet feels at this spectacle"—this though the "spectacle" includes the mystery of what the poet calls "an Assumption" that has both classical and Christian coloring as a marble figure "with the unripe breasts of the Virgin" ascends out of the ancient tomb to vanish in the sky, and though what the poet sees and feels in the presence of this mystery is rendered in language and imagery out of "The Book of James" (see *The Apocryphal New Testament*, 18:2), which of course may or may not be regarded as a mythical source depending on the character of one's persuasion.

[24] Vayenas himself (*The Poet and the Dancer*, p. 272) calls the relation between the ancient myth and "the experience" Joyce describes as "loose," and he adds that "at very few points could it be used as an interpretive analogy."

the poet employs at some moments in the sequence to create specific mythical episodes and simply abandons at other moments. Once the mythical dimension has been established by voice, image, and allusion, as it clearly is established in the early poems of the sequence, all that follows participates—often by way of tone and repeated motifs—in the poet's continuous parallel between contemporaneity and antiquity, whether or not the mythical dimension of the parallel is brought overtly to the surface.

The poem's "voice," its many-faced persona, is a principal manifestation of the myth's continuing presence. I indicated above that though the voice assumes several masks, it speaks with a consistent tone and in a consistent style, whether it expresses itself by way of the first person singular or the first person plural, whether it addresses a second person or describes a setting or narrates an action. Since I have already attempted to define the characteristic stance and attitude of this voice or persona, I need not offer further definition in this addendum, but I do want to emphasize that those who do not hear it speaking in its persistent tragic rhythms behind the various masks it assumes or through the various personal pronouns it adopts as it expresses its image of thirsting despair and forges its parallel between the ancient world of myth and the contemporary sorrow, are in danger of giving the poem a naive reading and finally of missing the beat of its heart—that particular beat which is one of the beneficial consequences of Seferis's assimilation of the "dramatic manner of expression" with its "elements of tragedy" that he acknowledges having discovered in Eliot just two years before he began to write *Mythistorima*.[25]

If the unifying tone of this voice does not come through clearly enough for those who have to hear it in translation, its continuity and its association with the volume's "certain mythology" are still persistently apparent in the imagery that gives the voice substance. The four poems in which Vayenas

[25] *On the Greek Style*, pp. 166-168.

finds "no mythical intimation" and which presumably refer "only to contemporary reality" may serve to illustrate my point. We discover in each of the four the same tone of voice that speaks in the overtly mythological poems (see p. 77 above for relevant examples), and we discover in each specific images that derive from the "mythical story" that the sequence tells: the voyage without end through a barren landscape and desolate seascape to search for the first seed or another golden fleece or the longed-for island home, the voyage first outlined in the opening poem of the sequence and rounded out in the fourth. No. 7 echoes No. 1 in the images of a "wind that blows and drives us mad," in its swan's wings, and most of all in the concluding question: "Who will accept our offering, at this close of autumn?" which carries us back to the "carved reliefs of a humble art" that the voyages of No. 1 brought back from their tormented, wounding journey, and the "idols and ornaments" drawn up to please our friends in No. 2. In No. 8, the contemporary voyage to one or the other of the Greek islands becomes part of the poem's mythical journey as the voyages of the first stanza find that they are traveling without a sense of direction or sense of touch to islands that remain just out of reach (the end of the voyage, Ithaca, is of course denied those weak companions who have fallen off the roof of Circe's palace in a drunken stupor or who have eaten the Oxen of the Sun, and these voyagers of No. 8 both recall the submissive voyagers of No. 4 and anticipate the "weak souls among the asphodels" of No. 24). In No. 10, along with the allusion to the Symplegades (through which Jason and the Argonauts had to pass in their quest for the golden fleece), we learn that those who find themselves in an arid landscape related to that projected by earlier poems in the sequence descend to contemplate "the broken planks from voyages that never ended," a distinct echo of the "voyages that did not end" in the earlier "Argonaut" section (No. 4) of the poet's mythical story. And even in what seems one of the most personal and lyrical interludes in the sequence, No. 15, the familiar "voice" of earlier sections concludes the poem with images equally familiar, as we hear him pitying "those, alone, who speak to cisterns and wells / and drown in the voice's circles" and "the companion who shared our privation and our sweat / and plunged into the sun like a crow beyond the ruins / without hope of enjoying our reward"—the companion here most surely bearing a "mythical intimation" as one of those Elpenorlike figures from the endless voyage of No. 4 who will be denied his Ithaca and his name in days to come, here "changed in keeping with the passing of time and the different conditions of our world," as the poet put it in his commentary on the character of the mythical figures in his work.[26]

The echoes of the poet's mythical voyage and its arid setting—its solitude, frustrated searchings, dubious offerings, unsatisfied nostalgia, and endlessness—are quite obvious in these four sections, if less directly mythologized than in some other sections. To ignore the latent—and sometimes not so latent—presence of the myth in these instances is to fracture the poet's intended coherence and continuity and to miss much of the text's final impact. But for me to labor the point further is to undermine the force and subtlety of *Mythistorima*. After some fifty years of life, the volume still projects, with its own simple if dramatic eloquence, the new territory that it charted for a continuous passage between ancient myth and contemporary history, as its title still so clearly signals.

[26] "A Letter on '*Thrush*,'" p. 501. For the full context, see the James Stone translation of the letter, cited in n. 6 above.

SEFERIS'S
"POLITICAL" VOICE

The funeral of George Seferis in September, 1971, proved to be a more or less spontaneous public event, not to say political demonstration, of a kind normally reserved in Greece for the passing of popular prime ministers, especially if at the time they are illegally out of office. The drama and symbolism of Seferis's funeral—thousands of young people raising the victory sign at the poet's grave, shouting "immortal," "freedom," "elections," and singing an early Seferis lyric set to the music of a former EDA deputy, Mikis Theodorakis— would surely have surprised the poet himself even more than it may have surprised his readers in the English-speaking world. Less than three years before his death, Seferis had declared, in one of the few interviews he allowed to appear during his lifetime (reprinted in its entirety as the postscript to this book):

> I am sorry to say that I never felt I was the spokesman for anything or anybody. . . . I've never felt the obligation. . . . Others think they are the voices of the country. All right. God bless them.[1]

As a diplomat sometimes at the center of political action, he inevitably felt a degree of tension between his public responsibilities and his more private obligation to his muse, as he

---

[1] See pp. 214-216 below for the context of Seferis's remarks.

reveals in a number of passages in his *Journal*.[2] But he struggled to keep the tension out of his work. When I once asked him if, as a practicing poet, he ever found his life in the diplomatic service a burden, he answered: "Only when my public life begins to enter my dreams. Then I know I've reached the danger point, and I do something about it. Take a vacation. Something."

That Seferis could become a symbolic political voice of a kind he never aspired to be, even resisted intellectually and psychologically during his long public career, serves to explain much about the political and cultural climate that surrounded his last years of uneasy retirement in Athens. It also serves to

---

[2] There are so many references to this tension in the poet's *Journal* over the years that those who know the full text in Greek will have no need for specific citation here, but it may be useful to point to several passages in that portion of the *Journal* that has appeared in English (*George Seferis: A Poet's Journal, Days of 1945-1951*, trans. Athan Anagnostopoulos, Cambridge, 1974), e. g., on p. 6, under "Monday, St. George's Day" [1945]: "I've made up my mind to do whatever I can to end this situation that has lasted now for seven years, the condition to which I have felt bound, obligated by the war. I did what I could, gave my very best in order to help. To keep on, I would have to enter politics actively, and I don't want that. I'll keep working for the only thing that I *myself* can do, that depends on me. All those days that went by (one month) I had to make a great effort to rid myself of the ropes which had cut into my flesh; a painful effort; I'm just beginning . . ."; and on p. 39, under "Saturday, October 5, Poros, Galini" [1946]: "I came here last Wednesday, when a long period of my life in service had come to a close—eight or nine years, starting from the period of the Anschluss. The Ministry has given me two months' vacation . . . I haven't been in a mood to turn to this notebook these days. All my dreams (those of sleep) are reenactments of my public life and my monologues (early in the afternoon today I took a long walk along the road to the monastery) are filled with utterances of this same kind. I carry much filth within me that must go . . ."; and, finally, on p. 191, under "Wednesday, November 8" [1950]: "Returning from Smyrna, I tried to approach a poem. As always here the gift of God is drowned in a pool of torpor. Furthermore, I need quadruple effort to do anything. Never before have I needed such will to write the twenty-five pages of Cappadocia—not even when I wrote the essay on *Erotokritos*, which had nonetheless plunged me into indescribable despair. No one can realize what difficult conditions I work under and how dearly I pay for my profession. . . ."

illuminate an aspect of both the man and his work that remains controversial, at least in Greece.

The vehemence of Seferis's refusal to act the spokesman in 1968 suggests a bitter history. In Greece, tradition has it that there must be a major poet on the scene—a poet laureate self-declared or popularly indicated—who is willing to serve as the voice of his country, and in years past one has always come forward to fill the need: Solomos, Palamas, and Sikelianos are the most obvious examples. After the death of the last in 1951, Seferis became, willy-nilly, the acknowledged heir to this tradition. He was Counselor of Embassy in London at the time, and during the decade that followed, as a member of the Greek delegation to the United Nations and as ambassador in London, he was frequently involved in the diplomatic negotiations over the Cyprus issue that darkened British-Greek relations throughout the 1950s. His direct participation in this area of international politics gave additional ammunition to those who wanted him to serve as the voice of Greece.

When Seferis published his 1955 volume of poems dedicated "To the People of Cyprus, in Memory and Love"—his first volume since the death of Sikelianos—critics in Greece, quick to dress him in the mantle of national poet, either celebrated the publication as an eloquent defense of Greek interests in the Cyprus dispute or criticized the poet for beginning to write what was understood to be propaganda in verse form. This response distressed the poet, and rightly so. The volume, which was in part the product of three visits to Cyprus between 1953 and 1955 while Seferis was an ambassador in the Middle East[3] actually presented poems very much in the mode of those he had been writing since the years immediately before and during World War II. With the exception, perhaps, of two poems, there is little in this work that might be called political, however one defines the term, and in these as well as others, the voice is essentially the same as that which we hear in many

[3] Specifically, ambassador to Lebanon, Syria, Jordan, and Iraq, with his headquarters in Beirut.

poems of *Logbook I* (1940) and *Logbook II* (1944), a view that the poet himself seems to have endorsed when he changed the original title of the volume, *Cyprus, where it was decreed . . .* (a fragment from Euripides's *Helen*) to *Logbook III.*

The two poems that might be considered exceptions are "Helen" and "Salamis in Cyprus," where one can discern a more than usually overt politico-historical coloring. Yet in the first of these, which invokes Euripides's version of the Helen of Troy story, the poet is careful to present his commentary on war and conflict through the agency of a persona wearing the mask of Ajax's brother Teucer. It is by way of this "persona," ancient exile in Cyprus where Apollo decreed that he should live and name a city "Salamis" in memory of his island home, that we learn about the old "idiocies of men / or of the gods" that caused the Trojan War and ten years of slaughter "all for a linen undulation, a filmy cloud, / a butterfly's flicker, a wisp of swan's down, / an empty tunic."[4] Teucer— in keeping with the legend that Euripides used in his play— has seen Helen in Egypt by the mouth of the Nile and learned that she never actually went to Troy herself, only a phantom image of her, and the Greeks thus fought for nothing, because "the gods wanted it so." The persona wonders if this is only a fable or if "mortals will not again take up / the old deceit of the gods" so that some future Teucer finds himself fated to hear "messengers coming to tell him / that so much suffering, so much life, / went into the abyss / all for an empty tunic, all for a Helen." This is no doubt meant as a comment on the conflict that tormented "sea-kissed Cyprus" at the time the poem was written, but it is a comment by implication

---

[4] The translation here was revised for *The Dark Crystal* (Athens, 1981 and Princeton, 1981, under the title *Voices of Modern Greece*) and also appears among the revised versions in the new (1981) edition of Seferis's *Collected Poems*, the source of other translations of Seferis in this essay. For the legend on which Euripides based his play, see the Loeb edition (London and New York, 1912) p. 463 ("Argument"). For a detailed account of the poem's ancient sources, see Katerina Krikos-Davis, "On Seferis' 'Helen,' " *Byzantine and Modern Greek Studies*, Vol. 5 (1979), pp. 57-76.

only, made entirely within the framework of Seferis's established dramatic and mythological modes. And in keeping with previous work, it is a meditation on war in general as much as a comment on a specific current conflict.

The second poem, "Salamis in Cyprus," is in a sense more overt in its commentary—and it is one of the two poems in the volume that the poet identifies specifically with a time and a place ("Salamis, Cyprus, November '53"), thus underlining the contemporary relevance.[5] Still, the poet's view of current events is presented through several strategies of indirection that not only save the poem from the taint of propaganda but serve to raise the poem's message to a level that transcends the particulars of a moment in history—the level that engages the general human predicament associated with war and political conflict throughout history.

The poet's message comes by way of several voices, in both monologue and dialogue form. The first voice we hear is that of the poet—or his contemporary persona speaking in the first person—describing a deserted beach, "covered with fragments or ancient jars," near Cypriot Salamis. As the persona stands there he is caught up by a sensual image of "young bodies, loved and loving ... throbbing breasts ... feet / fearlessly skimming the water, / and arms open for the coupling of desire" (one is reminded of Cavafy's "images of sensual pleasure" interrupting the poet's contemplation of shore and sea in "Morning Sea"). It is an image of vibrant young life, but it is invaded by an ominous voice described as "heavy like the tread of oxen," one that remains "there in the sky's veins, in the sea's roll." This voice brings word of life transformed by bitterness and evil and of the doom that lies ahead for the presumptuous mighty, as it invokes the historical context of both General Makriyannis's *Memoirs* of the Greek War of

[5] The other poem that Seferis identified by date and place in the first edition of the Cyprus volume is "Neophytos the Englistran Speaks," a satirical exercise with political overtones that concludes with a version of Othello's deranged: "You are welcome, sir, to Cyprus—Goats and Monkeys!"

Independence and of Aeschylus's *The Persians*, [6] in particular the speeches of the Persian Messenger describing the terrible destruction of the Persian fleet in the straits of the Greek island of Salamis and the slaughter of arrogant Xerxes's choicest troops on the island of Psyttalea fronting Salamis.[7] The voice, echoing Aeschylus, tells us that it doesn't take long for "the yeast of bitterness to rise," for "evil to raise its head" and "the sick mind / to fill with madness," the last a paraphrase of Darius's view that his son Xerxes must have been possessed by a "distemper of the soul," because "mortal though he was, he thought in his folly that he would gain the mastery over all the gods, aye even over Poseidon."[8]

The implied parallel between the Greek and Cypriot Salamis and the eventual doom of mighty powers given to hubris that the Aeschylean allusions point to are inescapable, but they are still implicit. And this implicit commentary continues as the poet-persona's voice returns with a recollection of "friends from the other war"—presumably the Second World War— "those who fell fighting and those who fell years after the battle," some of these no doubt British friends who were once allies of the Greeks but whose country is now among the antagonists of Greece and Cyprus both. Another voice breaks in, appropriately that of Commander Lord Hugh Beresford who fell in the battle of Crete and who offered a wartime prayer (paraphrased in the poem) which underlines the perennial vices that war engenders and which expresses the hope that these may be driven out of his ship:

---

[6] See the Greek edition of Seferis, ed. G. P. Savidis (Athens, 1972), p. 344, and Vayenas, *The Poet and the Dancer*, pp. 213-214 and p. 319, n. 53 and 56.

[7] The phrase "there is an island" that concludes this passage in the poem and that is repeated as the poem's last line opens the Messenger's account of the Psyttalea slaughter, l. 447.

[8] See *The Persians*, ll. 744-751. The translation by Herbert Weir Smyth is from the Loeb edition. See also ll. 813-822.

"Lord, help us to keep in mind
the causes of this slaughter:
greed, dishonesty, selfishness,
the desiccation of love;
Lord, help us to root these out . . ."

The poem concludes with a dialogue between two uniden-
tified voices, the one taking the position that "it's better to
forget; / talking doesn't do any good," because those in power
cannot be changed and will not listen anyway, and the second
voice answering from the larger historical perspective, again
with an echo from Aeschylus's *The Persians*: the mighty who
tried to shackle the Hellespont in their hubris[9] and to conquer
Greece eventually heard the terrible news of their defeat by
much smaller forces in the battle of Salamis, and the messenger
who brought that news is still with us, still swift, however
long his journey.

The message of "Salamis in Cyprus" is as overt as Seferis
permitted himself to become in his mature poetry, yet it is
still presented by way of several masks and by way of historical
allusion. If the voice here—really the product of an interplay
of voices—can be called "political" at all, it would have to
be designated as such in only the broadest terms, those that
suggest a discourse outside the political arena, where the per-
spective is that of a brooding conscience which sees a tragic
course for those in power who play the god arrogantly by
imposing their will on others assumed to be weaker—those
who act with the old presumptuous pride known as hubris—
and which sees a process of general corruption and alienation
attendant on war, a "desiccation of love," whatever the spe-
cific political context.

This is not a perspective that is encountered for the first
time in *Logbook III*, nor are the strategies of the two so-called
political poems in this volume an innovation. Both have their
origins in the poetry Seferis wrote immediately before, during,

[9] Ibid., ll. 745-749.

and after the Second World War. The brooding voice, the perspective, the historical reminiscing and alluding that signal the poet's roused conscience are manifest, for example, in the poem "The Last Day," written in February, 1939, as Europe was moving toward the brink of a general war and Greece was in the third year of the Metaxas dictatorship:

A funeral march meandered through the thin rain.
How does a man die? Strange no one's thought about it.
And for those who thought about it, it was like a
    recollection from old chronicles
from the time of the Crusades or the battle of Salamis.
Yet death is something that happens: how does a man die?
Yet each of us earns his death, his own death, which
    belongs to no one else
and this game is life.
The light was sinking over the clouded day, no one decided
    anything.
The following dawn nothing would be left to us, everything
    surrendered, even our hands,
and our women slaves at the springheads and our children
in the quarries.

Though the poem opens with a mention of soldiers presenting arms and ends with the laconic bit of dialogue " 'I'm sick of the dusk, let's go home, / let's go home and turn on the light,' " both of which establish a contemporary context, there is no direct reference to the political circumstances of the moment.[10] The issue is the larger one inspired by that

[10] The influence of current historical context in establishing the political implications that some readers seem inevitably to bring to Seferis's work is illustrated by the surprising response—at least surprising to me—that this poem elicited when I read it before an audience made up of both English- and Greek-speaking students at Harvard in December of 1968, that is, a year and a half after the junta of colonels established their dictatorship in Greece. Without meaning to suggest the particular relevance of individual poems, I had dedicated my reading of the English text (Seferis read the Greek originals without commentary) to my childhood friend, Pavlos Zannas, who was in

moment: how does a man die properly?—an issue that goes back to *Mythistorima* (e.g., No. 22). A sense of doom hangs over the poem, but it is conveyed, again, through historical allusion which serves to link this moment to the history of the race: to the fate that Hector says may lie in wait for his wife Andromache after the defeat of Troy, when she will surely be taken to Argos to "ply the loom at another's bidding, or bear water from Messeis or Hypereia"[11] against her will, and to the fate of the Athenian prisoners sent into the Sicilian quarries after the disastrous expedition of 415 B.C. There is no more overt comment in the poem: it is a moving if subtle expression of the same prophetic sense of his country's fate that the poet conveys by the famous lines in "The King of Asine" (finished in January, 1940) that picture the country "like a large plane-leaf swept along by the torrent of the sun / with the ancient monuments and the contemporary sorrow," or the image of companions "on the blackened ridge of Psara" calling for help in January of 1942, during the worst winter of the Occupation, while the poet—and his persona Stratis Thalassinos—finds himself in exile and thoroughly alienated among the agapanthi of Transvaal.[12]

---

prison at the time for having distributed, along with others, a pamphlet proclaiming the Greek dictatorship illegal (see p. 116 below). This may have set a tone for the reading that I hadn't quite anticipated. Suddenly, when I reached the end of my English version of this pre-Second World War poem and read the lines "I'm sick of the dusk . . . / let's go home and turn on the light," the hall was filled with what seemed a spontaneous burst of applause; and then someone at the back of the room yelled: "Let's turn on the light in Greece," and there was even louder applause clearly meant to indicate a communal commitment to resistance against the dictatorial regime then in the second of its seven years in power.

[11] Trans. A. T. Murray, Loeb ed. (London and Cambridge, Mass., 1960), p. 295.

[12] The poem is entitled "Stratis Thalassinos among the Agapanthi." The line "on the blackened ridge of Psara" repeats the opening line of Solomos's famous "The Destruction of Psara," which commemorates the razing of the island of Psara and the massacre of its people during the Greek War of Independence. A translation of the full Solomos poem appears in a note to Seferis's poem, *Seferis: Collected Poems*, p. 541 (under "287").

Again, at the end of the war, when the poet has returned to the Italian coast near Salerno to await repatriation to Greece, he has occasion in "Last Stop" to review the experience of the war years in the same voice that we will hear at times in the Cyprus volume, strongly influenced by the voice of Makriyannis, whose earthy honesty about the heroic and unheroic side of both war and postwar politics is clearly Seferis's model:[13]

We come from the sand of the desert, from the seas of Proteus,
souls shriveled by public sins,
each holding office like a bird in its cage.
The rainy autumn in this gorge
festers the wound of each of us
or what you might term differently: nemesis, fate,
or simply bad habits, fraud and deceit,
or even the selfish urge to reap reward from the blood of others.
Man frays easily in wars;
man is soft, a sheaf of grass,
lips and fingers that hunger for a white breast
eyes that half-close in the radiance of day
and feet that would run, no matter how tired,
at the slightest call of profit. . . .

And as the poet-persona continues to meditate on his particular experience of war, what he calls "the thinking of a refugee, . . . of a prisoner, . . . of a person when he too has become a commodity," we find him admitting not only to saying "the same thing over and over again" but saying it by way of fables, parables, and allusions, his normal mode for rendering history that is too complex and ominous for any ordinary political discourse—the telling allusion here again from Aeschylus:

[13] Several quotations from Makriyannis appear in the poem, including "fraud and deceit" in the passage that follows, from *Memoirs* (Karavia ed.; Athens, n.d.), III, 416.

And if I talk to you in fables and parables
it's because it's more gentle for you that way; and horror
really can't be talked about because it's alive,
because it's mute and goes on growing:
memory-wounding pain
drips by day drips in sleep.

The allusion to the *Agamemnon* again raises the poet-persona's images of personal experience and personal conscience to the level of the perennial, even the prophetic, where horror is seen to breed horror and where the pattern of human frailty, violence, and corruption that the poem reviews is seen to be part of the recurring human predicament that Aeschylus was among the first to explore.

The poet's ambitious postwar meditation touching on "war, destruction, exile," the long poem *"Thrush,"* is too intricate and varied to lend itself conveniently to the kind of outline I am engaged in here (and in any case I comment on it in an earlier essay),[14] but again the reader will find voices, fables, images, allusions, and a persona that present the poet's meditation on contemporary experience in a dramatic and allusive form that anticipates the mode of the poems in the Cyprus volume, not least of all the two I have discussed in some detail. Given Seferis's long commitment to transforming politico-historical occasions by subtle means into the broader perspective that I have outlined, it is not surprising that the poet was upset by the narrow response to the Cyprus volume (apparently even among some of his more sensitive and friendly critics who expressed their views in private),[15] nor is it surprising that his irritation might lead him to dismiss any sort of public role for the kind of poet he chose to be. At the same time, Seferis remained Greek through to his bones. As has been suggested elsewhere,[16] he continued to make out of his personal experience metaphors that served to define the char-

[14] See Sef. 1, above.
[15] So the poet once told me in conversation.
[16] In the Introduction to *Seferis: Collected Poems*, pp. xiii-xv.

acter of his nation, and he continued to render his broad vision through those elements most representative of his nation: its landscape, its legends, its demotic tradition in literature, its mythic and historic past. This is true to an extent even of his most private volume, significantly entitled *Three Secret Poems*, where the voice is a degree more obscure and elusive than what we have seen and where allusions to contemporary history are strictly veiled. The volume's "secrecy," its privacy, were perhaps in part the product of a retrenchment after the poet's rather unhappy and unfair experience with the Cyprus volume, and it was more than ten years in the making, appearing in print just a few months before the military coup of April 1967 that established the seven-year dictatorship under the juntas of Papadopoulos and Ioannides.

Seferis's irritation regarding the public role he was supposed to play as heir to Sikelianos became acute after the Nobel Prize award of 1963 moved him onto an international stage. He was now not only unofficial poet laureate but the first Greek Nobel laureate of any kind, with a fame that quickly spread far beyond national boundaries. And if those of his countrymen who never read poetry sometimes confused him with a Greek soccer star of similiar name and renown, many of those who knew better began to look to him for the sort of prophetic leadership that nobody else was providing after the military dictatorship of 1967 gave even the most conservative intellectuals cause for despair. But whatever Seferis's private sentiments, he remained adamant at first about avoiding public pronouncements. In the same 1968 interview quoted above, I asked him whether or not he felt any responsibility, given his unique position as Greece's only Nobel laureate, toward younger poets and the cultural life around him. Seferis, catching what he took to be a barb in the question, answered rather petulantly:

> . . . the Nobel Prize is an accident, no more than an accident. It's not an appointment. And I have no feeling that I have been appointed to any sort of function. . . . I

don't recognize the right of anybody to take you by the back of your neck and throw you into a sort of ocean of empty responsibilities. Why, that's scandalous after all.[17]

These remarks were made toward the end of Seferis's three-month term as fellow of the Institute for Advanced Study in Princeton. It was an interlude free of the external tensions that he had felt building up around him in Athens after April 1967, but not entirely free of the inner tensions that any poet of his sensibilities would carry with him wherever he might seek relief, especially one so acutely sensitive to his nation's pulse and so conscious of the dangers that lay in censorship and in the arbitrary regulation of the mind's enterprises. (Hadn't he and other intellectuals encountered the same sort of despotism under the Metaxas dictatorship and the German Occupation?)

His inner discomfort came to the surface at a reading that he gave at the Y.M.H.A. Poetry Center in New York in December of 1968. During the discussion period several people in the audience questioned him directly about his attitude toward the régime in Greece. Seferis evaded the questions by implying that they were inappropriate for the occasion, which hardly satisfied the more fanatic element in his audience and clearly served to distress the poet himself, because he pursued the matter at a small dinner following the reading. His actual motive for not answering such questions, he said in private, was that he did not consider it proper for him to criticize his government while he was in a foreign country, safely outside the range of the government's displeasure (and, presumably, its possible revenge).

Some who heard this explanation thought it equally evasive, but Seferis gave the lie to all doubting some three months later, after his return to Athens, when the pressure he had been under found its liberation in the dramatic statement that he issued on March 28, 1969:

[17] For the context, see pp. 213-215 below.

Long ago I resolved to remain out of the country's internal politics. This did not mean ... that I was indifferent to our political life. For years now I have in principle abstained from such matters. But what I said in print up to early 1967 and the stand that I have since taken (for since freedom was muzzled I have published nothing in Greece) showed clearly enough what my attitude was.

Now for some months, however, I have felt, within me and around me, that more and more it is becoming imperative for me to speak out on our present situation. To put it as briefly as possible, this is what I would say. . . .[18]

Throughout the morning of the 28th, word had spread among Seferis's friends in Athens that the poet had smuggled some sort of recorded statement out of the country for broadcast over the BBC at 9:00 that evening, and there was much activity through the day by those in the know searching out a good short-wave set and a safe gathering place, as though the broadcast was one of those that used to come through to Greece under the Nazi Occupation, when the voice of courage from England was the only free voice left to feed the morale of a harassed and starving people. The voice that came over the set that evening was heavier than Churchill's, certainly slower and less overtly rhetorical, yet it carried some of the same prophetic resonance, the same invocation of doom, as it spoke of the "state of enforced torpor," "the stagnant waters" in which the ideals and intellectual values fought for in World War II were now being submerged, and of the tragedy that "waits at the end, inescapably" for dictatorial régimes that have a seemingly easy beginning. The poet concluded:

I am a man completely without political ties and I speak without fear and without passion. I see before us the precipice toward which the oppression that covers the

[18] The translation, supervised by the poet, is that which was issued to the press. The complete statement appeared in English translation in the July 1969 issue of *Encounter*.

108

land is leading us. This abnormality must come to an end. It is the nation's command.

Now I return to silence. I pray to God that never again may I find myself under such compulsion to speak.

If Seferis spoke without fear and passion, there was enough of both in the audience listening to him to bring on some restless hours following the broadcast. What would the régime do now? Arrest him? Imprison him? Send him into exile? Take away his home? Seferis himself told me some time later that each of these possibilities had crossed his mind as he prepared to break his silence, but real as they may have seemed at moments, all such thoughts had to be dismissed.

"I ended up ready for anything but expecting nothing," he told me. "The only emotion I felt once I'd made the decision to speak was intense liberation." And virtually nothing is what he got—at least in the beginning. Several friends were daring enough to cruise by his home late that evening to see how many police and plainclothes men a resistant poet merited in the eyes of the régime, but all that showed in the street outside his house were strolling lovers looking for a dead-end retreat.

The first official response was a series of harsh, sometimes incoherent editorials on the front page of the leading pro-government newspaper, the aim to discredit this Seferiadis ("Seferis" is a nom de plume) as a communist sympathizer. One piece made out that Mr. Seferiadis had visited and congratulated a leading ELAS guerrilla leader in his mountain hideout during the Occupation, but it proved to be the wrong Seferiadis, as the paper itself had to admit on being informed by one of its own who had an unrevised memory that George Seferiadis was abroad at the time with his country's Government-in-Exile. Several days after the broadcast a plainclothes man did show up at the Seferis home to make some inquiries—questions that seemed to be directed toward verifying the existence of a poet by some such name—but the plainclothes man remained so mild, so painfully ill at ease, that he ended up apologizing to the maid for having intruded on her hospitality.

The one substantial indication of the régime's displeasure came some weeks after the government newspapers decided to let the case against Seferis rest. Anticipating a trip abroad for a medical checkup with a specialist, the poet applied to the Ministry of Foreign Affairs for a renewal of his diplomatic passport, which, by convention, was his for life as a former ambassador. The régime's foreign minister, Pipinellis, who had been the poet's colleague for years, personally issued a note denying the passport renewal. After protests from various sources, Seferis was informed that Pattakos's Ministry of the Interior was prepared to issue him a regular passport if he were to appear personally and request it. Seferis vowed that he would never submit to that kind of humiliation because it would bring discredit on all former civil servants who had served their country in a capacity similar to his. The one exception to this posture that he allowed, privately, was the possibility of traveling outside Greece for urgent medical assistance—an exception that he reluctantly had to invoke two years later, during the spring before his death.

If the official attitude toward Seferis in the months following his statement was essentially one of pretending that he was too senile to be taken seriously, the attitude of intellectual circles in Athens, from students to fellow writers, was one of homage that soon approached adoration. "The Poet" became "Our Poet." It was not merely that Seferis had finally accepted with full heart his expected role of laureate-spokesman, but as the first independent man of mind with the courage to speak out on an international stage against the régime and the drift of its ambitions, he served to free others with less opportunity for courage and a smaller platform. The immediate result of his influence was the coming together of a group of writers, with disparate political affiliations but a common distaste for the dictatorship, a rather motley but nevertheless committed intellectual underground that produced a strong anti-régime statement supporting Seferis's position, and, eventually a volume of anti-régime stories, poems, and essays entitled *Eighteen Texts* (Athens, 1970; Cambridge, Mass., 1972), with the lead contribution Seferis's first publication since his 1966 volume, a poem called "The Cats of Saint Nicholas," set off by a pointed epigraph that again invoked Aeschylus's *Agamemnon*:

> But deep inside me sings
> the Fury's lyreless threnody:
> my heart, self-taught, has lost
> the precious confidence of hope . . .

The poem itself, a kind of fable, is in the mode we would expect from our review of the "political" voice in Seferis's earlier work—in fact the poet indicated that a draft of the poem was written for the Cyprus volume but was finally not included in it.[19] One might therefore see any political relevance that the fable could be said to have as appropriate first of all to the Cypriote context, but there was no indication of this at the time of publication. The setting of the poem is a ship passing through Cypriot waters, near "Greek's Rock," a presumed birthplace of Aphrodite, and the Cape of Cats, home of a medieval monastery that housed an army of cats, heroic cats who managed during a great drought to keep the Cape clear of venomous snakes by giving relentless battle, day and night, stopping only for their evening meal before returning, wounded and crippled, to the combat:

". . . Supper done, the bell would sound again
and out they'd go to battle through the night.
They say it was a marvelous sight to see them,
some lame, some twisted, others missing
a nose, an ear, their hides in shreds.
So to the sound of four bells a day

---

[19] This emerged from a conversation with the poet at the time he asked me to translate the poem into English for publication in *Encounter*, July, 1969.

months went by, years, season after season.
Wildly obstinate, always wounded,
they annihilated the snakes; but in the end they disappeared;
they just couldn't take in that much poison.
Like a sunken ship
they left no trace on the surface:
not a meow, not a bell even.
Steady as you go!
Poor devils, what could they do,
fighting like that day and night, drinking
the poisonous blood of those snakes?
Generations of poison, centuries of poison."
"Steady as you go," indifferently echoed the helmsman.

Immediately on publication in *Eighteen Texts*, the poem
was taken to be a fable that pointed to the possibility of heroic
resistance to the oppression of the Colonels. And the poet did
nothing to inhibit this widely accepted reading. The only other
poem he allowed to appear under the dictatorship (and this
abroad, first in English translation), " 'On Aspalathoi' . . ."
gave further support to this revived "political" reading of his
work because it seemed to have an even more pointed—though
still allusive—relevance to the dictatorship, in this instance
suggesting what Seferis's statement had already prophesied:
that doom lay in store for tyrants who ruthlessly imposed
their arrogant will on others. The poem opens with a stanza
of lyric description of Sounion on a spring day, the aspalathoi
with their huge thorns and yellow flowers already out and
ancient columns in the distance like the strings of a harp still
vibrating. Then:

Peace.
What could have made me think of Ardiaios?
Possibly a word in Plato, buried in the mind's furrows:
the name of the yellow bush
hasn't changed since his time.
That evening I found the passage:

112

"They bound him hand and foot," it says,
"they flung him down and flayed him,
they dragged him along
gashing his flesh on thorny aspalathoi,
and they went and threw him into Tartarus, torn to shreds."

In this way Ardiaios, the terrible tyrant,
paid for his crimes in the nether world.

March 31, 1971

The quality of the "resistance" volume in which Seferis's "Cats of Saint Nicholas" appeared was inconsistant, as one might expect of a collection made up largely out of materials that the contributing writers had on hand at the time and that had been produced under the stress of censorship. But the publication of it nevertheless called for some courage, given the régime's capricious modes of exercising reprisal for published opposition: everything from heavy irony to long jail sentences. Its response in this instance was an attempt to discredit the volume on aesthetic grounds ("bourgeois" literary criticism always seems to be among the first weapons that Right or Left dictatorships claim the competence to wield in self-defense), and an attempt, also, to exploit the publication of it under censorship as an example of the government's tolerance. The effect was to make it an immediate best-seller (in Greek terms) and to inspire two additional collections that were increasingly overt in their satirical comment on conditions in Greece. The effect was also to put Seferis at the center of opposition to the régime's control over the intellectual life of the country, to make him gradually the unacknowledged leader of dispossessed students and the silent voice of those with no public outlet for their own brooding sense of injustice—until the feeling he had engendered found an ultimate release in the surprise of his funeral.

Indications of the latest role that had been given him began to appear during the agony of his last days in the intensive care ward of Evangelismos Hospital. When an emergency call went out to friends and relatives for blood after the second operation to relieve the poet's hemorrhaging ulcer, dozens of unknown young people appeared out of nowhere to give their blood, and during the weeks of waiting for the end—the poet suffering from increasingly critical complications—others, unidentified, came to sit in the dreary waiting room beside those close to the poet, as though a secret honorary guard. A representative of the Junta also appeared eventually, the head of the new Ministry of Culture and Science, and after paying his respects to Mrs. Seferiadis, reputedly sat down and wept— until he was asked to try please to control his emotions because it was difficult enough for those who had been controlling theirs all this time with more than one cause for weeping. There was talk in the waiting room, and at private meetings elsewhere, about who ought to be asked to deliver what sort of eulogy, and what might be the most effective way of dramatizing Seferis's recent political role, and what international political figures might be encouraged to take part. There was also more restrained talk about what might be legitimately done to prevent the poet's funeral from being exploited for political purposes of any kind. Mrs. Seferiadis wanted it to remain an essentially private occasion in the small chapel where she had married the poet, with no eulogies or other manifestations except for a few words from a student at the grave. And the poet himself remained unconscious of the debate going on around him, almost totally immobile during the final stages, except very near the end when a young girl was wheeled into the ward beside him for her own battle with death. He was then seen to turn his head for the first time in days and look at her with wide unmoving eyes, as though feeding for his last breath on what youth and beauty there was still in her to give.

I rely on the witness of others for images of the funeral itself (I had to leave Athens at the end of that summer, some days before the funeral, to return for the fall semester at Princeton). One such witness who reached the small church an hour and a half early was the poet's friend Philip Sherrard, co-translator of our collected edition of his poems. Sherrard reported to me in a letter:

> The church was more than half full when I arrived and the police were already in position. . . . I looked about at the people gathered there—several hundred already, there must have been—and suddenly I became alarmed. I thought I'd made a mistake: among all those faces, of seated or standing people, there was not one I recognised: literally not one. Then I looked at the "honorary guard" of four men standing around the coffin. Again, completely unknown faces. Was I in the wrong chruch? But for whom else could so many have gathered? I tried to find the name of the church, but couldn't see it anywhere. I was ashamed to ask my neighbours: who is being buried? I stayed put: it couldn't be anyone else. Then I saw how foolish my fears about being respectfully dressed had been; half the crowd around me were wearing the most casual clothes, shirts and dresses of gay colours, tieless, jacketless. It was strange: rather like a student's gathering at the end of term. Which in a way it was, because 80 percent of the people must have been students, with some fine faces among them, of both sexes. I wondered what lay behind it all—behind, or within, this youthfulness, I mean—and I remembered Yanni Peltekis saying a few months before he died that this generation of Greek youth was the best Greece had known since the age of Pericles (though I've doubts about the virtues of the youth of that particular age). Will anything come out of it?

When the Archbishop, Ieronymos, appeared and was greeted by "a barrage of coughs and hisses" from those who considered him a Junta collaborator, and when the voices outside the church drowned out the liturgy in their recognition of a wreath allegedly sent by Andreas Papandreou (though others report the wreath to have been from a group of prisoners in Tripoli), the political coloring of the occasion became blatant, to the gratification of some and the dismay of others. There were wreaths from the Left and the Right, including one from the exiled king. There were also wreaths from political prisoners held in Trikala, Corfu, and elsewhere, ribboned with quotations from the poet's work that had been removed during the night only to be restored at dawn: "In a little while we will see the almond trees blossoming," and "The axle creaks, the axle burns, when will the axle burst into flame?" And one "To Uncle George, from his six Salonika nephews" (the "nephews" all once promising democrats of the center and still relatively young, but sentenced to serve a part of their youth in jail for distributing pamphlets proclaiming the Junta illegal during the first months after the coup).

The way to the cemetery, crowded by thousands, also roused confused emotions in those who knew the poet. The novelist Kay Cicellis described the liberating side of it:

> The moment we emerged from the church into the open was overwhelming. We suddenly became aware of the enormous waiting crowd—then, quite spontaneously, untidily but unanimously, they all began singing [the Seferis lyric set to music by Theodorakis]. And with the song rising up, up, the sadness began to lift too and we floated along as if on air, the stream widening as we went along until it flooded the cemetery. Have you ever seen that quiet, tidy, civilised cemetery crowded? People converged to the grave from every alley, every pathway ... with rallying cries, more songs.[20]

Some of those already at the grave were overwhelmed in another way by those flooding into the cemetery to climb any available object for a better view. Sherrard reports that "hundreds of photo-reporters, followed by hundreds of others, scrambled over the marble tombs, swarmed up the marble crosses, even perched in the branches of the cypress trees." The Greek friend with him "lost his temper as some oaf, mounting a tomb, butted him in the face with his bottom.

---

[20] From a letter to me shortly after the funeral.

'Donkeys,' he shouted. 'Why are we donkeys?' the man on the tomb asked. 'Because you put your ass in my face.' "

Another witness reports that there was almost open violence (so rare among civilians in Greece) when one group of people pushing their way through to the grave encountered another group pushing furiously in a different direction and accused the latter of illiteracy. It turned out that the "illiterate" group was indeed unaware that a great poet was being buried because they were very busy trying to get their own dead body (belonging, some said, to a popular goatherd) through that mass of literate mourners and into a grave some distance beyond the poet's. The one person who might have brought these contending factions together with an amused chuckle was the one person there who had to miss it all.

What kind of funeral would it have been had the circumstances leading up to it been otherwise—had the poet not been compelled, by his conscience and the tragic destiny of his nation, to play a role he never wanted to play? Was the political gesturing of so many who knew the poet largely through a popular song and a courageous act really appropriate, really justified? Philip Sherrard offers a plausible answer in his letter:

> Somewhere within this scene the real dirge was going on, the dark note. Even the [Theodorakis] song had something of it now: "but the sea breeze blew / and the writing vanished." And—who knows?—perhaps that life had changed at the heart of itself, or at least gone elsewhere. Anyway, how else could these young people express themselves? Yes, perhaps it was justified. But it was impossible not to wonder how many of them would have been there had it not been for politics, had it all taken place when there was no need or pressure to make a demonstration of this kind. . . . It was impossible not to wonder how many of them who followed this dead man and who were capable of making this political gesture, perhaps even of sacrificing their lives, at a moment of excitement or violence, in the name of a "cause" or a

"movement"—how many of them were capable of making that greater sacrifice of devoting years of their lives to patient study of, and reflections on, those inner currents of beauty and meaning which finally alone make it bearable to go on living at all? Because that surely was his example, his lesson. . . . "What is going to become of this race?" our Greek friend said. "It's missing exactly what he had in such abundance: the control that comes with breeding."

Another answer might be that given the kind of race it is and the kind of poets who emerge as the voice of that race, it is as natural that Seferis be celebrated in his death for an act of conscience as it is that Aeschylus be honored in his epitaph for the valor he showed in the grove of Marathon. And there is a third answer, one that might have brought on the kind of enigmatic smile characteristic of Seferis when he considered it diplomatic to remain silent and not commit himself in company, or when he wanted to underline a bit of self-irony: if the tone and the range of the event that his funeral became were perhaps out of key with the strictly controlled political voice of his poetry and the equally controlled manner of his life as a public servant, it nevertheless demonstrated that, in Greece, poetry finally matters in a symbolic way even to those who don't read it, and the poet's voice has some hearing when it is considered to count most. Seferis once told me that he thought a poet had the right to earn at least as much as a shoemaker. He might have added, with that smile, "and the death he earns ought to bring him as much attention as that of a popular soccer player or at least a popular goatherd."

The Voices of
Elytis's *The Axion Esti*

The response of Greek readers to Odysseus Elytis's most ambitious poem, *The Axion Esti*, was ambivalent during the first few years after it appeared in Athens in late 1959 to end more than a decade of silence by a poet then considered to be Greece's best hope among the "younger" generation of poets to follow George Seferis.[1] Though the poem earned the First National Award for Poetry in 1960 and was widely read during the years that followed, the attitude of leading critics remained mixed. A similar ambivalence was also evident in the response of some English-speaking readers to the two sections of the poem that appeared in this country and England during the 1960s.[2] For those brought up on the post-Eliot/Pound mode—or on the Cavafy/Seferis mode—the poem was seen to be excessively rhetorical and subjective, at times too obviously programmatic in its formal and thematic projections, at other times too obscure.

Given a commitment to these anti-rhetorical modes, one

---

[1] Yannis Ritsos, who has now emerged as the other distinguished heir to Seferis, was still suffering at that time from either unpremeditated ignorance on the part of the Greek and foreign literary establishment or what some have seen as a politically motivated conspiracy of silence which prevented his just recognition (thoughts that I outline more fully in the opening paragraphs of the Greek version of the essay on Ritsos below).

[2] "The Genesis" in *Poetry* (October, 1964) and "The Gloria" in *Agenda* (Winter, 1969), both translated by Edmund Keeley and George Savidis.

---

could find ample ground for regarding the poem as overblown in many of its parts, perhaps even in its central intentions. But this is not the only commitment that governs modern poetry, certainly not in the case of the modern Greek tradition. Those readers familiar with twentieth-century Greek poetry can discern a direct line from the rhetorical modes of Palamas and Sikelianos to those of *The Axion Esti*, modes that many Greek readers would consider as characteristic of Greek verse in this century as the more frugal, controlled expression of Cavafy and Seferis. During the 1970s there was increasing evidence in the response of English-speaking readers—particularly among those practicing poets who turned (or returned) to the surrealist movement of the early twentieth century for their principal inspiration—that the poem spoke with some power and originality even in translation. And of course the audience for the poem has grown, at least in the United States, since Elytis won his Nobel Prize in 1979.[3]

My argument here is that there is no single mode in the poem but several modes and a variety of voices—some more objective and dramatic than others, some more effective than others, but serving to shape an impressive poetic statement in their totality—and that even the most subjective and rhetorical of the poem's voices really should be judged within a relevant context: that phase of the modern Greek tradition which foreshadows Elytis's use of an enlarged first person, his most

---

[3] The 1974 translation of the full poem by Keeley and Savidis under the title *The Axion Esti*, originally published by University of Pittsburgh Press in a bilingual edition, was reissued by the same press at that time in an English only paperback edition, and Kimon Friar's 1974 translation of selected poems of Elytis, *The Sovereign Sun*, which included selections from *The Axion Esti*, was also reissued in 1979. The first edition of *The Axion Esti* to appear in England was a reissue of the Keeley-Savidis Pittsburgh volume by The Anvil Press in 1980. The same press, in collaboration with Penguin, published *Odysseus Elytis: Selected Poems*, ed. Edmund Keeley and Philip Sherrard, in 1981, a selection that includes a sampling of the Keeley-Savidis version of *The Axion Esti* (this volume was published in the United States at the same time by Viking/Penguin). The translations offered in this essay are from the University of Pittsburgh/The Anvil Press edition.

controversial voice. For those English-speaking readers without easy access to the work of Palamas and Sikelianos, it may be helpful to approach the poem not with reference to the post-Eliot/Pound mode but with reference to those poets in our tradition who engaged in an enterprise parallel to that of Elytis, specifically Walt Whitman and Dylan Thomas. Both these poets project a first-person voice that usually manages to transcend the subjective and rhetorical trappings that come with it, sometimes in a manner that anticipates Elytis's first-person speaker in portions of *The Axion Esti*. When Whitman sings, in "Song of Myself, 16," that

I am of old and young, of the foolish as much as the wise,
Regardless of others, ever regardful of others,
Maternal as well as paternal, a child as well as a man,
Stuff'd with the stuff that is coarse and stuff'd with the
     stuff that is fine,
One of the Nation of many nations, the smallest the same
     and the largest the same,
A Southerner soon as a Northerner . . .

his large first-person voice is meant to rise above the subjective syntax and to speak for the nation, for the proposed national sensibility that the "I" is intended to represent; and it is partly the rhetorical tone of the passage that forces the reader to accept this grand design.

Elytis attempts the same kind of representation through his first-person speaker in several of the Psalms of Part Two, "The Passion," for example, in Psalm III:[4]

RICHES you've never given me,
devastated as I've always been by the tribes of the Continents,
    also glorified by them always, arrogantly!

or in Psalm V:

---

[4] The designation "Psalm" is explained in the general note on "The Passion" that appears in *The Axion Esti*, trans. Keeley and Savidis.

MY FOUNDATIONS on mountains,
and the people carry the mountains on their shoulders
and on these mountains memory burns
like the unconsumed bush.

Here the first-person voice speaks for the nation more than
for the self: those riches never given, and the devastation by
"tribes of the Continents," are attributes that belong not so
much to a personal as a national predicament; and "my foun-
dations" become the country's foundations when the moun-
tains that hold them are raised on the shoulders of "the people."
The rhythm, as in Whitman, is that of a rhetorical progress
from "I" as persona to "I" as metaphor for a general sensi-
bility.

In those instances when Elytis's first-person voice speaks in
a more overtly personal context, his mode appears closer to
that of Dylan Thomas, whose work also reveals a parallel
handling of imagery. The opening lines of Thomas's "Fern
Hill," for example, remind us of lines in part one, "The Gen-
esis":

Now as I was young and easy under the apple boughs
About the lilting house and happy as the grass was green,
    The night above the dingle starry,
        Time let me hail and climb
    Golden in the heydays of his eyes,
And honored among wagons I was prince of the apple towns
And once below time I lordly had the trees and leaves
        Trail with daisies and barley
    Down the rivers of the windfall light.

"The Genesis" opens as follows:

    IN THE BEGINNING the light And the first hour
            when lips still in clay
            try out the things of the world
        Green blood and bulbs golden in the earth

——
122

And the sea, so exquisite in her sleep, spread
unbleached gauze of sky
under the carob trees and the great upright palms
        There alone I faced
        the world
        wailing loudly

Both poets offer a persona who speaks out of personal past history, childhood in the case of Thomas and infancy in the case of Elytis. But the objective of this personal evocation is to provide a context for the creation of the brave new world that each persona discovers during the innocence of his early life. The focus is not on autobiographical detail but on those elements that make the world surrounding the persona green and golden, before the progress of time intrudes to bring a consciousness of the fall from grace—the knowledge of death in Thomas and of evil in Elytis—that change early Eden into the harsher world of later years. The subjective voice again serves a broader, metaphoric vision; the rhetorical tone, even the conceits ("prince of the apple towns," "unbleached gauze of sky") again seem appropriate in elevating the ordinary to the level of wonder, specifically, the wonder that comes with "trying out the things of the world" in a state of innocence.

These parallels illustrate two forms of the first-person voice in *The Axion Esti*, forms that fall between what Palamas called the personal and the temporal, or "lyricism of the I" and "lyricism of the *we*."[5] When Elytis allows the personal, or the self, to dominate the more general group consciousness, he is clearly less successful, as in Pslam X of "The Passion," where the persona's defensiveness under attack by "the young Alexandrians" seems to border on paranoia. And he is also less successful when his persona takes on the role of prophet, turning from the re-created world before him to visionary abstractions, as he sometimes does in passages of the Reading

[5] See Christopher Robinson's illuminating discussion of *My Poetic* in "Greece in the Poetry of Costis Palamas," *Review of National Literatures* (Fall, 1974), pp. 42-45.

called "Prophetic" and in the late Psalms (for example, "I see the coherence of secret meanings," or "Blessed, I say, are the potent ones who decipher the Undefiled"). The first-person voice appears inevitably to speak with the greatest conviction and force when it is discovering or celebrating or even challenging the symbols of "this small world the great" that are rooted in the Greek reality, whether of landscape, recent history, or literary tradition—all of which evoke a shared, group response and therefore transcend the overly hermetic.

The same criterion applies to the first-person voice of the numerous intricate Odes of "The Passion," a voice that is in one sense the most subjective and rhetorical that we hear in *The Axion Esti* but that is at the same time the most formal, confined within the limits of a lyrical frame created by strict metrics and frequent refrains. It is a voice clearly meant to sing, and we permit it some of the license this intention presupposes. But again, to the extent that the rhetorical "I" of these Odes "takes the shape of my native country" (as the poet himself puts it in Ode j), it escapes an excess of self-consciousness and promotes some of the finest lyrics that Elytis has written. To the extent that it speaks privately or with a tone of self-righteousness ("Betrayed, I remained on the plain, alone, / Stormed, I was taken in the castle, alone, / The message I raised I endured alone! ") or through slogans ("In the desolate and empty city / only the hand remains / To paint across the great walls / BREAD AND FREEDOM") or in "prophetic" abstractions ("But then, at the sixth hour of the erect lilies, / When my judgment will make a crack in Time, / The eleventh Commandment will emerge from my eyes: . . ."), it rings rather hollow, the product not so much of the poet's mature, liberated spirit as of his programmatic attempt to present grand themes.[6]

A related esthetic can be brought to bear on the more objective voices that emerge in *The Axion Esti*, and they are several. One index of the sophistication of this poem, of the

---

[6] An outline of Elytis's program, taken from his unpublished commentary on the poem, is offered in the Notes to the English version of *The Axion Esti* (Pittsburgh, 1974).

progress in method that occurred during the years of silence that preceded it, resides in the poet's "dramatic manner of expression" (to invoke again the phrase Seferis offered in designating what he had learned first of all from reading Eliot's *The Waste Land*)[7]—an expression that often finds embodiment in characters some distance from the poet himself and his persona. The first such character to appear is "the One I really was, the One of many centuries ago, / The One still verdant in the midst of fire, the One still tied to heaven" in "The Genesis," a kind of alter ego who acts as the creator of the infant poet's green world. This voice utters some of the best lines in the poem, lines that are effective exactly because they evoke a recognizable landscape, a poetic image of Greek reality, while at the same time dramatizing the infant poet's emerging sensibility:

And ample the olive trees
    to sift the light through their fingers
    that it may spread gently over your sleep
and ample the cicadas
    which you will feel no more
    than you feel the pulse inside your wrist
but scarce the water
    so that you hold it a God and understand the meaning of
        its voice
and the tree alone
    no flock beneath it
    so that you take it for a friend
    and know its precious name
sparse the earth beneath your feet
    so that you have no room to spread your roots
    and keep reaching down in depth
and broad the sky above
    so that you read the infinite on your own[8]

The experiment in dramatic expression extends, in "The

---

[7] *On the Greek Style*, p. 167.
[8] From the third "hymn," discussed in more detail below.

Passion," to a series of prose poems called Readings, where the speaking voice is essentially that of a narrator, though the narrative focus shifts from the point of view of a participant in the action to that of a more distant observer and, finally, to that of the "poet-prophet" mentioned above. The voice is most alive in the early Readings, when Elytis succeeds in creating a tone that is organically related to his subject and to the image of experience he wishes to project, without the intrusion of explicitly subjective overtones. In the First and Second Readings, for example, the unidentified narrator, a soldier participating in the historical moments described (both during the Albanian campaign of 1940-1941), speaks in a colloquial language that provides verisimilitude in that particular context and that also subtly echoes the colorful demotic of a great nineteenth-century narrator, General Makriyannis, whose *Memoirs* described the Greek War of Independence and its political aftermath.[9] The relation of World War II to earlier Greek history in terms of an engaged perspective is thus established by narrative tone as much as by the kind of direct allusion—too direct for my taste—that invokes heroes out of the past to travel in the company of our contemporary soldiers.[10] In the best of the Readings, tradition becomes an organic element of the language celebrating tradition.[11]

The voice in the concluding section of the poem, "The Gloria," is perhaps the most consistently effective in *The Axion Esti*. Here the poet overtly assumes the stance of celebrant, but in general he allows the world he is celebrating to speak for itself. Except for the refrains "PRAISED BE" and "HAIL," he remains outside the context he projects, and the refrains simply establish a frame of intention, a celebrative tone, for his evocation of all that he finds in "this small world the great" which is most worthy of praise. The proof of worthiness is left to the images created, without any subjective pressure from poet or persona; the value of the world rendered depends

[9] See above, Sef. 3 and below, E 2.
[10] As in the fifth paragraph of the First Reading.
[11] This is a theme explored more fully in the essay that follows.

on the degree to which we the readers find the various images of it convincing—and most of them prove to be so. This suggests a truly liberated strategy, one that serves to invoke the best of Elytis's early work but now reinforced by a mature command of plotting, of decorum and aptness in the progression from one image to the next, values sometimes slighted in the early Elytis. Perhaps more important, in some passages of this section, the poet succeeds—as his predecessor Seferis so often does—in conveying the mythological dimension that pervades the details of contemporary life in Greece without pressing the case through overt comment or excessive allusion to literary sources (and the allusions given us are usually to a relevant native tradition, rarely to arbitrarily imported foreign sources). In the following passage, for example, gods and heroes from the Greek past are brought subtly into the contemporary landscape by way of a sudden metaphor linking a tree trunk with the goddess of fertility and vegetation who presumably animates it, by way of a compound epithet, by way of a name carrying echoes of Homer, by way of the intermingled whispering of deities and the natural element they inhabit, all made to seem casually at home in the island world that the poet is celebrating:[12]

> Hera of the tree's ancient trunk
> the vast laurel grove, the light-devouring
>   a house like an anchor down in the depths
> and Kyra-Penelope twisting her spindle
>
>   The straits for birds from the opposite shore
> a citron from which the sky spilled out
>   the blue hearing half under the sea
> the long-shadowed whispering of nymphs and maples

Throughout most of this final section of the poem, Elytis is observing first of all, observing and re-creating, selecting

[12] Also explored more fully in the following essay.

details that will move the reader to a recognition and letting any attendant thematic or ideological overtones come as they may. The picture is all, and when it is right, it can startle the reader with a new perspective on the hauntingly familiar:

> PRAISED BE the wooden table
> the blond wine with the sun's stain
> the water doodling across the ceiling
> the philodendron on duty in the corner . . .

> PRAISED BE the heatwave hatching
> the beautiful boulders under the bridge
> the shit of children with its green flies
> a sea boiling and no end to it . . .

> THE ISLANDS with all their minium and lampblack
> the islands with the vertebra of some Zeus
> the islands with their boat yards so deserted
> the islands with their drinkable blue volcanoes

The only faltering in "The Gloria" is that which we have seen in other sections: a weakness for vague abstraction in those few moments when the poet attempts to rise above the world before him to the region of absolutes and general principles. In the closing lines of this section, he juxtaposes representations of the "Now" and the "Forever" in a sort of coda to the whole poem. Neither plane, as rendered here, moves the heart or even the mind to the kind of discovery effected by the specific images we have seen. And this rhetorical mode of evocation serves to diffuse and intellectualize what has so far been poetically concrete:

> Now the hallucination and the mimicry of sleep
> Forever forever the word and forever the astral Keel

> Now the moving cloud of lepidoptera
> Forever the circumgyrating light of mysteries

> Now the crust of the Earth and the Dominion

Forever the food of the Soul and the quintessence . . .

Now the amalgam of peoples and the black Number
Forever the statue of Justice and the great Eye . . .

The poem ends: "and Forever this small world the Great!"
Indeed. But as the best passages in the poem demonstrate, the
eternal dimensions of this small world are most convincingly
established when the greatness of it is celebrated with a lower
case "g." This is the poet's strongest impulse in the poem,
and it is what makes *The Axion Esti* both a major stage in
the poet's development and a major contribution to the mod-
ern Greek tradition in poetry.

ELYTIS AND

THE GREEK TRADITION

When most English-speaking readers hear the phrase "the Greek tradition," the image that immediately comes to mind is that of classical Greece—Plato, Aristotle, the Greek dramatists, Thucydides—or perhaps pre-classical Homer and the great epics, or even behind this, strange gods and their bizarre metamorphoses. Readers in the West would naturally assume that this ancient tradition has a particular relevance for Odysseus Elytis, born in Crete in 1911, trained in Greek and French literature, and sufficiently well-known in the West to have won the 1979 Nobel Prize in literature. And every educated Westerner knows that the Greek tradition did not stop with Euripides and Plato, or even with the Hellenistic poets thereafter, but traveled from Alexander's empire to Rome and on to Constantinople over many centuries. Yet I suspect that few of the English-speaking readers who have begun to become acquainted with modern Greek literature through an interest in one or the other of the Greek writers now earning an international audience realize that some of the best poets and critics in Modern Greece feel at least as much kinship with their medieval Byzantine heritage and the Christian tradition in literature as they do with its pagan antecedents or the subsequent incursion of Renaissance influences from the West. Elytis is clearly among these.[1] Furthermore, when one

[1] The most articulate and learned presentation of the case for Greece's need

speaks of tradition to a contemporary Greek poet, tradition without any qualifications, one is likely to find oneself understood to mean the demotic tradition that shaped the language of contemporary poetry, beginning in medieval times and progressing continuously—if sometimes haltingly and under attack[2]—through the folk-song culture and what is known as the Cretan Renaissance and on into the 19th century demoticism of Solomos, Makriyannis, and Palamas, finally to the work of those writers most familiar to current readers in the English-speaking countries: Cavafy, Kazantzakis, Sikelianos, Seferis, Ritsos. And this latest phase of the three-thousand-year long Greek tradition can also be seen as a vital influence on the work of Elytis, as I hope to demonstrate below with specific reference to Sikelianos and Seferis.

Along with a failure to recognize the full character and range of the tradition most relevant to Elytis, English-speaking readers have been heir to several presuppositions that have provided them with a distorted image of the poet. One that still endures especially in England, the Western country that has been slowest to appreciate Elytis, is that the Greek poet remains more French than Greek. Robert Graves is reported to have said some years ago: "Elytis is just Eluard pronounced with a Greek accent. Just another French surrealist really." I will return to this peculiar—and admittedly unverified—representation in due course. A second, more generous distortion is that which has been promoted by English and American philhellenes who see Elytis in the same light that they have sometimes seen his country, that is, as open territory for discovering their less inhibited and more hedonistic selves (one is reminded here of Henry Miller's related theory that getting to know Greece is "like falling in love with one's own divine

to reassert the vitality and relevance of the Christian—as against the Renaissance—tradition is made by the Greek poet-critic Zissimos Lorenzatos in his book *The Lost Center.*

[2] See "Solomos' *Dialogos* and Dante," ibid., for a succinct history of the changing fate of the spoken language as the language of literature in Greece.

image").[3] The philhellenic representation I have in mind is expressed most poignantly in Bernard Spencer's "A Spring Wing," written during World War II, a poem that celebrates the nostalgia for Greece which many of us in the West who have come to know that beautiful country begin to feel with the first cruel stirring of April year after year. As Spencer puts it: "Greece, I have so much loved you / out of all reason, that this unquiet time— / its budding and its pride, / the news and the nostalgia of Spring— / swing towards you their tide"; and when spring shakes the windows of Spencer's wartime London, making the doors whang to and the sky shine like knives, it is specifically Elytis that he finds before him "uttering the tangle of sea, the 'breathing caves' / and the fling of Aegean waves."

Elytis, Poet of the Aegean Islands, its maidens, its sun and sea, its liberating light, poet of youth and optimism, of lyricism, fancy, lightheaded surrealist excess. A true image in some measure, but this is the Elytis of Spencer's works and days, not ours; though the distorted image shaped by nostalgia has some relevance to the work Elytis published before and during World War II, it is a partial representation at best. Yet "Poet of the Aegean" is still the most familiar of the clichés one hears in the West when Elytis's name comes into the conversation or the literary exercise, and the second most familiar is that which Graves is said to have accommodated for Elytis's denigration: just another French surrealist spelled with a sigma—this again a cliché engendered by Elytis's earliest work.

If we grant that Elytis is the "Poet of the Aegean" in the lighter aspect of his sometimes truly dark vision, the question of French surrealist influence still remains to be explored. I want to focus for the moment on the early verse, where the influence is presumably the most glaring. As I have said elsewhere,[4] what Elytis actually offered in the two volumes he

[3] *Greece* (New York, 1964), p. 45.

[4] In the portion of the Introduction to *Six Poets of Modern Greece* having to do with the Elytis selection in that volume.

published during the late thirties and early forties was a sur-
realism that had a highly personal tone and a specific local
habitation, neither of which had much to do with French
sources. The tone was celebrative, adoring, even ecstatic; the
habitation, what appeared most often as the object of his
ecstasy, was the particular landscape projected by his native
land—and I have in mind a landscape that includes charac-
teristic figures as well as a poetic rendering of those vistas
familiar to every tourist who has fallen in love even briefly
with what the light does to the mountains and the ruins and
the waters of almost any place far enough from Athens to be
still habitable. In my early commentary on Elytis I suggested
that the evocation of landscape and climate through surrealist
images is not only everywhere apparent in Elytis's early verse,
but the surrealist evocation focusses so consistently on the sea
and the sun as to suggest a kind of pagan mysticism, a panthe-
ism, a worship of the gods of water and light. But what I want
to emphasize here is that however freewheeling the images
may appear to be, however fanciful the poet's juxtapositions,
however cunning the sudden metamorphoses he offers—a girl
becoming an orange, another's morning mood becoming a
mad pomegranate tree, summer becoming a naked ephebe—
his surrealism is always rooted in a literal native landscape
that is identifiable within the poem. Take the most flamboyant
of his early surrealist exercises, "The Mad Pomegranate Tree,"
with its "saffron ruffle of day / Richly embroidered with scat-
tered songs," and the tree of the title "adorn[ing] itself in
jealousy with seven kinds of feathers, / Girding the eternal
sun with a thousand blinding prisms," finally "fluttering a
handkerchief of leaves of cool flame"—even here, where the
poet's imagination seems to have taken on the wings of Icarus
so as to fly perilously close to the sun, it is the *Greek* sun his
hubris courts, as we see in the final stanza, where the Feast
of the Virgin on August 15, that day which marks the close
of summer for vacationing Greeks, becomes at least one of
the rhetorical excuses offered for this mad tree's uncontained
hilarity and generosity:

In petticoats of April first and cicadas of the feast
    of mid-August
Tell me, that which plays, that which rages, that which
    can entice
Shaking out of threats their evil black darkness
Spilling in the sun's embrace intoxicating birds
Tell me, that which opens its wings on the breast of things
On the breast of our deepest dreams, is that the mad
    pomegranate tree?[5]

Or to take another early example, the poem called "Drink-ing the Sun or Corinth" from the 1943 volume *Sun the First,* where the celebration of landscape seems almost a religious exercise:

Drinking the sun of Corinth
Reading the marble ruins
Striding across vineyards and seas
Sighting along the harpoon
A votive fish that slips away
I found the leaves that the sun's psalm memorizes
The living land that passion joys in opening.

I drink water, cut fruit,
Thrust my hand into the wind's foliage
The lemon trees water the summer pollen
The green birds tear my dreams
I leave with a glance
A wide glance in which the world is re-created
Beautiful from the beginning to the dimensions of the heart!

The title and the first line are enough to establish the precise local habitation that I referred to earlier, but even if we didn't have Corinth, most of the other details in the landscape are familiar enough to travelers in Greece: the marble ruins, the

---

[5] Translations of Elytis's work are from *Odysseus Elytis: Selected Poems,* ed. Edmund Keeley and Philip Sherrard (New York and London, 1981).

vineyards, the lemon trees. And even in the concluding image, which, in its surrealist mode, has the world "re-created / Beautiful from the beginning to the dimensions of the heart"—a seemingly arbitrary bringing together of time and space in a manner that Breton would have approved—even here there is a hidden echo of Seferis in the phrase "dimensions of the heart," and behind Seferis's "from the down of the kiss to the leaves of the heart," of the "Erotikos Logos," Seferis's own source in folk songs and the *Erotokritos*, that 17th-century Cretan epic-romance which has been so influential in the modern Greek tradition. Elytis constantly translated his early surrealism into the language of his country's landscape and literary heritage in ways that might escape readers in the West brought up on the classics and European literature and little firsthand knowledge of the Greek tradition that is most relevant to modern Greek poetry.

The best statement on how Elytis actually accommodated French surrealism to his own purposes, how he brought it into just relation with the Greek tradition that he considered his most vital resource, comes from the poet himself in an interview he gave Ivar Ivask.[6] Elytis's statement brings into question the characteristic image of Greece that is found in most Western readers, and he indicates why he felt that surrealism could serve to counteract this image, which he apparently saw as a major distorting influence within his own country, an attempt by intellectuals foreign and domestic to impose the Renaissance on territory that had in fact survived without it during the four hundred years of Turkish occupation and that revealed its true roots elsewhere:

I and my generation—and here I include Seferis—have attempted to find the true face of Greece. This was necessary because until [our generation] the true face of Greece was presented as Europeans saw Greece. In order to achieve

[6] First published in the special issue of *Books Abroad* devoted to Elytis (Autumn, 1975) and reprinted in *Odysseus Elytis: Analogies of Light*, ed. Ivar Ivask (Norman, Okla., 1981), pp. 7-15.

this task we had to destroy the tradition of rationalism which lay heavily on the Western world. Hence the great appeal of surrealism for us the moment it appeared on the literary scene. Many facets of surrealism I cannot accept, such as its paradoxical side, its championing of automatic writing; but after all, it was the only school of poetry—and, I believe, the last in Europe—which aimed at spiritual health and reacted against the rationalist currents which had filled most Western minds. Since surrealism had destroyed this rationalism like a hurricane, it had cleared the gound in front of us, enabling us to link ourselves physiologically with our soil and to regard Greek reality without the prejudices that have reigned since the Renaissance. The Western world always conceives of Greece in the image created by the Renaissance. But this image is not true. Surrealism, with its anti-rationalistic character, helped us to make a sort of revolution by perceiving the Greek truth. At the same time, surrealism contained a supernatural element, and this enabled us to form a kind of alphabet out of purely Greek elements with which to express ourselves. . . .[7]

And he goes on to speak specifically of his interest in coordinating the surrealist belief in the value of the senses with the Christian notion of sanctity, of elevating the senses "to a level that is sacred."[8]

It is perhaps in this conjunction that we find the clue to what Elytis means by the phrase "purely Greek elements." What he has in mind, it would seem, are not so much those elements promoted by the classicist offspring of the Renaissance as those promoted by Byzantium, by the modern Greek folk tradition, and by the demotic tradition from the Cretan Renaissance on through the 18th and 19th centuries. At least it is this phase of the Greek tradition that is most apparent in his major work, *The Axion Esti*, published in 1959, a work

[7] *Analogies of Light*, p. 7.
[8] Ibid., p. 8.

136

that shows the poet translating his early surrealist mode into a new style that is usually more subtle, usually more controlled, than what we have seen in his early poems, yet that still retains a lyrical vitality and a cunning arrangement of evocative images.

Before I resume my exploration of those traditional elements that count most for Elytis, I want to refer the reader one passage from the first section of *The Axion Esti* that can serve to illustrate the change in style that I discern in this poem. The passage quoted above (E1, p. 125) once again takes us to an Aegean landscape—or seascape, more exactly—and to the Cyclades Islands; and again the focus is on a rendering of those elements most worthy of celebration because they contain an eternal majesty, or as close to it as we mortals can experience in what Elytis calls "this small world the great." But the evocation here is not so much through startling images, fanciful juxtapositions and the like, as it is through the naming of significant details and through a dramatic mode that depends on a play of voices. We first hear the voice of the infant poet awakening to the knowledge of his country and the shapes in it that will constitute the material of his poetry. Then we hear the voice of his spiritual advisor and alter ego (for lack of a better definition), the "One of many centuries ago" who helps to create this brave new world for the poet in rhetoric that here seems entirely appropriate to the context (as it is not at moments in the early verse and even at other moments in this poem). The new world here emerges detail by bright detail in a manner that Pound of the early *Cantos*—anyway those with passages of lyrical geography—might have admired.

To return to our theme, I think the mix of traditional sources—traditional but non-classical or Renaissance sources—that helps to create the texture of the poem is most evident in its middle section called "The Passion," where we find constant echoes of the Greek Orthodox liturgy, of folk songs, of Dionysios Solomos and other 19th-century demotic literature, as well as a number of experimental verse forms that are clearly meant to link this poem to the Byzantine and post-Byzantine tradition. For example, in the prose poem that appears under the heading "Second Reading" (the title itself establishes a liturgical analogy), we find first of all a rendering of a brief moment in the Albanian Campaign of 1940-1941 against the invading forces of Mussolini, that heroic action in which the outnumbered Greeks pushed the Italians at least part of their way back home and in which the poet participated as a young officer. But the rendering is in a style that has distinct Biblical echoes, and at the same time it reflects—as was indicated in the previous essay—a calculated attempt by the poet to invoke the style and verisimilitude of General Makriyannis's famous *Memoirs* of the Greek War of Independence, a beautifully honest, down-to-earth prose document in a version of 19th-century demotic, one that required the illiterate general to become an autodidact in the written language and that George Seferis described as being "like an old wall in which, if one looks closely, one can trace every movement of the builder, how he fitted one stone to the next, how he adjusted every effort he made to what had gone before and was to follow after, leaving on the finished building the imprint of the adventures of an uninterrupted human action."[9] The text in translation cannot possibly convey all the rich echoes of Makriyannis's style that color the original, but a few lines of "Second Reading" may serve to suggest the subtle fusion of past and recent present that makes *The Axion Esti* a moving contemporary document in its best moments, a document that carries forward the tradition of national lyricism inaugurated by Dionysios Solomos early in the 19th century:

> In those days, at long last, after three full weeks, the first mule drivers reached our territory. And they told us a lot about the towns they'd passed through—Délvino, Saints Saránda, Koritsá. And they unloaded their salt herring and biscuits with an eye to finishing up as soon as possible and taking off. Because they weren't used to this booming

---

[9] *On the Greek Style*, pp. 31-32. Makriyannis's relation to some of Seferis's own poetry is illustrated above, pp. 99-100, 104.

from the mountains, it scared them, and so did the black
beards on our wasted faces. . . .

Elytis's emphasis on Byzantium and the demotic tradition,
especially effective in the kind of fusion this passage reveals
(anyway in the original Greek), does not by any means pre-
clude his use of classical and pre-classical sources, least of all
in the period under consideration (what he himself calls, per-
haps a bit self-consciously, his "middle period"). It is a matter
of degree, and his reticence in this connection reflects, I think,
his feeling that other modern Greek poets have depended too
much on the ancients in creating their image of contemporary
Greece. He has even implied that some, as a consequence of
their neo-classicism, may have earned a broader audience out-
side Greece than he himself has earned (or had earned until
his Nobel Prize). In the interview with Ivar Ivask, Elytis re-
marks:

> I have never employed ancient myths in the usual manner.
> No doubt it is advantageous for a Greek poet to employ
> ancient myths, because he thus becomes more accessible
> to foreign readers. A Greek poet who speaks of Antigone,
> Oedipus, et cetera, moves in an area which is well-known;
> through these mythical figures he can comment on con-
> temporary events. This was done by Sikelianos and, above
> all, by Seferis. In the case of Seferis it was almost natural,
> because he was influenced not only by his own Greek
> heritage but also by the manner of Eliot. Ritsos, too,
> especially in his latest period, employs figures from my-
> thology and Greek tragedy. I have reacted against this,
> often quite consciously, because I thought all this was a
> bit too facile, yes, even in the theatre. Many French and
> other European writers have, as you know, adapted the
> Electra myth, among others. Since my chief interest was
> to find the *sources* of the neo-Hellenic world, I kept the
> mechanism of mythmaking but not the figures of my-
> thology.[10]

[10] *Analogies of Light*, pp. 10-11.

Elytis goes on to explain that he has in mind the kind of metamorphoses we've already identified in "The Mad Pomegranate Tree" and "Body of Summer." But as he himself indicates, this technique which he labels "myth-making without evoking any mythical figures," is chiefly to be found in his early work. As his poetry matures, I see his use of ancient sources closely approaching the method of Sikelianos and Seferis, as I hope to illustrate below. And in certain passages of *The Axion Esti*, the ancient gods and their habitations, even the mythical figures in Homer, are not only hovering in the background of his verse but sometimes appear overtly. I refer the reader again to the following passage from the third section of the poem:

> Hera of the tree's ancient trunk
> the vast laurel grove, the light-devouring
>   a house like an anchor down in the depths
> and Kyra-Penelope twisting her spindle
>
> The straits for birds from the opposite shore
> a citron from which the sky spilled out
>   the blue hearing half under the sea
> the long-shadowed whispering of nymphs and maples

This passage reveals something other than myth-making through metamorphoses in the manner of the ancients. Here the mythic figures of Hera, Penelope, and the whispering nymphs come directly onto Elytis's stage. But the important point, as I suggested in the previous essay, is that they are made to seem entirely at home in the contemporary setting that the poet hymns in the poem's third section, appropriately called "The Gloria" (it is in this section of *The Axion Esti*, incidentally, that Elytis comes closest to realizing his aspiration of elevating the senses "to a level that is sacred"—to quote from the interview—because "The Gloria" is an extended hymn of praise that sings the holiness of those things in this world that most satisfy the senses, or those things that best unite the "now" and the "forever," as the poem phrases it).[11] The ancient tree-trunk in this passage can be seen as a legitimate, natural modern residence for godly mystery, as Kyra-Penelope is a perfectly legitimate modern name for the faithful old woman one sees in the rural doorways of Greece still making yarn from wool—if not actually weaving a winding sheet—while waiting for her husband to come home. And those nymphs appear casually among living trees, their traditional habitation, trees that are as natural to this white midday landscape as all the other elements that serve to define this poet's "small world the Great."

Elytis's mode of introducing mythic figures naturally into a contemporary setting is, to my mind, very reminiscent of Sikelianos's mode, and though Elytis may be reluctant to think so, he may well have learned something from Sikelianos about how to use his ancient mythic sources without making the mythology seem a rather alien intrusion, as it often is in French and Anglo-American literature, sometimes even in the work of those who practiced, in the early decades of this century, what Eliot called the "mythical method."[12] Eliot himself is a case in point. There are certain passages in *The Waste Land*, for example, where a figure out of Greek mythology will appear a bit awkwardly, a bit bookishly, in a contemporary London setting to comment on the local scene in a way that promotes irony more than anything else: a tongue-in-cheek revelation of the disparity between the high style and manner of the ancients and the rather sordid preoccupations of modern urban citizens—and Eliot's ambition in the poem is clearly not limited to irony, especially at those moments when Tiresias is the speaker. Eliot tells us in a note to the following passage that Tiresias is "the most important personage in the poem," and "what Tiresias *sees*, in fact, is the substance of the poem":

[11] This aspect of the poem is discussed more fully above, pp. 126-129.
[12] See above, pp. 74-75.

141

At the violet hour, when the eyes and back
Turn upward from the desk, when the human engine waits
Like a taxi throbbing waiting,
I Tiresias, though blind, throbbing between two lives,
Old man with wrinkled female breasts, can see
At the violet hour, the evening hour that strives
Homeward, and brings the sailor home from the sea,
The typist home at teatime, clears her breakfast, lights
Her stove, and lays out food in tins.
Out of the window perilously spread
Her drying combinations touched by the sun's last rays,
Stockings, slippers, camisoles, and stays. . . .[13]

Our first response to this passage and the lines that follow
it is to smile at Eliot's wit, and there is also something in that
smile occasioned by our finding the noble Tiresias forced into
alien territory to play the blind voyeur so that he can "see"
not the cruel fate of Oedipus but the quick seduction—"un-
reproved, if undesired"—of this indifferent London typist by
the "young man carbuncular." Our response to Sikelianos's
use of mythological figures in a contemporary context is rather
different. Compare, for example, the stanzas from Sikelianos's
"Pan" quoted on pages 46-48 above, stanzas written just a
few years before Eliot wrote *The Waste Land*. As I indicated,
Sikelianos's poem opens with what seems a characteristic lyr-
ical rendering of the contemporary Greek landscape and sea-
scape in the mode of those poems of his in which he offers a
subjective, often rhetorical celebration of the natural world
that Elytis will later celebrate in a surrealist mode. But we
saw that the natural world of "Pan" served as a mask for the
supernatural world and that the flock of goats "plummet[ing]
headlong" down the hillside on the shore opposite Salamis
became an occasion for the kind of mystery that could plau-
sibly show us the herd's lord and master metamorphosed into
the god Pan, with his identity designated by the title alone.

[13] *The Complete Poems and Plays, 1909-1950* (New York, 1952), pp. 43-
44.

Unlike Eliot's use of Tiresias, there is no hint of irony in Sikelianos's mythological apparition and no commentary from the mythical figure that underlines the disparity between past and present—what can sometimes seem an almost comical disparity. The unstated mystery of Pan's appearance at noonday on the seashore near Eleusis, home of the ancient Mysteries, emerges quite naturally out of the poet's native landscape, where, as I suggested, ancient presences still survive in the names of places and of the people who live there and in the very language that the poet uses to describe his setting. The poet thus needs no literary allusions to sources in his own or more remote traditions in order to dramatize his belief that the ancient pastoral gods still inhabit the territory he chooses to celebrate.

The surviving remnants of the ancient Greek world in language and setting clearly provide advantages for the contemporary Greek poet who wishes to demonstrate the relation of the modern world he lives in to its historical and legendary antecendents. This advantage worked well not only for Sikelianos but also for Seferis (see Sef. 1; Sef. 2), and I think Seferis was also among those predecessors in Greece who influenced Elytis in his use of traditional Greek sources and in his development of a personal voice. For one, he provided a model for the progress from French symbolist and surrealist expression to the kind of expression that can be said to reflect what Elytis called "the true face of Greece." In Seferis's case the progress was indeed aided, as he himself implied (see above, pp. 77-78), by his discovery of Eliot's poetry in 1931 and his response of the English poet's "dramatic manner of expression" and his representation of "thirsting despair" through "actual human character"—and one should add: human character often clothed in mythological dress, alien or otherwise.

There are several texts in Seferis that might serve to illustrate the early shaping of the model I have in mind. Perhaps the most obvious is "The Mood of a Day,"[14] written a few years before Seferis read Eliot, a poem that reveals the Greek poet's

---

[14] *Seferis: Collected Poems*, pp. 469-471.

close affinity to the surrealists during the first phase of his career and that also demonstrates what Elytis will later see as his affinity to Seferis. The first three stanzas of this poem are dominated by images that in their rather violent yoking together of disparities would have appealed to the surrealists André Breton and Paul Eluard, for example, the "marble setting" of September, the windows and doors opening their mouths like wild animals, love cutting time in two and stunning it, and boredom spreading like a drop of ink on a handkerchief. And the same mode carries over to the fairly arbitrary logic of the progression between stanzas which leads us finally from the tired man laying out cards in the mess and monotony of his room to the concluding image of a fated vessel out of Poe[15] traveling the seas with a dead captain and dead crew on board as though compelled by some inevitable destiny beyond mortal control or understanding, the ship's rigging filling with pride among the flashing dolphins and only the smiling mythical mermaid and a single forgotten sailor still in evidence to witness the ship's mysterious course.

What is the significance of this apparently doomed voyage? We don't really find out until several years later, shortly after Seferis picks up a volume of Eliot in the midst of a London fog and feels himself transported back to the imagery of his childhood by the vision of a lovely bow forging slowly ahead in Eliot's poem "Marina": "What seas what shores what grey rocks and what islands / What water lapping the bow / And scent of pint . . ." etc.[16] This vision, and the subsequent discovery of Eliot's dramatic manner of expression by way of actual human character, sometimes with mythic overtones (Seferis cites specifically the passage in *The Waste Land* where Stetson is addressed as the speaker's companion in the ships at Mylae)[17]—these discoveries lead to Seferis's crucial 1935 poem in twenty-four parts, *Mythistorima*, where a central

[15] As is indicated by the epigraph to the poem.
[16] *On the Greek Style*, pp. 166-167.
[17] Ibid., p. 168.

image (sometimes an aspect of the volume's central drama) is
a voyage that has no end through an arid seascape and where
one of the central characters is a kind of modern Odysseus
trying to return home to a world of beautiful islands and
blossoming almond trees that are just beyond reach, the voy-
age taking place in a ship made of rotting timbers manned by
a crew of weak, submissive companions given to hubris and
hedonistic excess (see Sef. 1, Sef. 2). Seferis thus moved from
his early surrealist expression of thirsting despair in the man-
ner of "The Mood of a Day" to a more subtle and dramatic
expression of the same theme, one that exploits Greek sources
in landscape, language, and mythology very much in the tra-
dition of Sikelianos's "Pan." As we have seen,[18] Seferis offers
us a landscape and seascape immediately recognizable by any
contemporary traveler passing along the coast of Greece, as
in Sikelianos's poem and in the passage from "The Gloria"
quoted above. Seferis's setting is often a relatively barren one—
a few rocks, a few pines, empty cisterns, a solitary chapel, a
whitewashed hut, all much tormented by maddening heat and
wind and the absence of water—and some readers might be
tempted to see its origins in Part V of *The Waste Land* were
it not a setting entirely characteristic of what that reader would
encounter among the smaller, virtually uninhabited islands of
the Cyclades or the Saronic Gulf. And it is in this kind of
realistically rendered contemporary landscape that Seferis's
ghosts from the ancient past are made to appear, sometimes
by allusion, sometimes by way of the setting's legendary or
historical associations, sometimes by a familiar image from a
mythical story he has told elsewhere or the name of a familiar
character in that story (e.g., Elpenor)[19] or a familiar word
with ancient connotations (e.g., "angel-messenger").[20] It is a

[18] Above, in Sef. 1, pp. 1-3 and Sef. 2, pp. 78-80.

[19] As is illustrated above, in Sef. 1 and in Seferis's "A Letter on '*Thrush*,' "
pp. 502-503.

[20] The problem the translator faces in rendering the various associations
of Seferis's "Ton angelo," which opens *Mythistorima*, is discussed in "On

mode at times clearly related to that of Elytis's "Hera . . . Kyra-Penelope" stanzas.

Sikelianos and Seferis thus seem to me the two immediate predecessors of Elytis in the Greek tradition, who guided him most on his way toward developing a voice that could hold the Greek past and present in just balance, specifically through their mode of bringing myth effectively into a contemporary context. And they did so not so much through a re-creation of classical works or by "speak[ing] of Antigone, Oedipus, et cetera" (to use Elytis's own phrase for it) as through the creation of a contemporary image of Greece and a moment of contemporary drama or mystery that—naturally, plausibly, usually without underlining or overt commentary—is subtly made to reveal its mythical presences and aura out of the ancient Greek tradition in the manner we have seen. I think the best example of an equally effective and subtle merging of the lingering ancient Greek past with its more accessible present in Elytis's mature work is the 1960 poem called "The Autopsy," from the volume, *Six and One Pangs of Conscience for the Sky*":

And so they found that the gold of the olive root had dripped in the recesses of his heart.

And from the many times that he had lain awake by candlelight waiting for the dawn, a strange heat had seized his entrails.

A little below the skin, the blue line of the horizon sharply painted. And ample traces of blue throughout his blood.

The cries of birds which he had come to memorize in hours of great loneliness apparently spilled out all at once, so that it was impossible for the knife to enter deeply.

Probably the intention sufficed for the evil

Translating Cavafy and Seferis," *Shenandoah* (Winter, 1972), pp. 40-41, and in an interview with Warren Wallace, *Translation Review*, No. 11 (1983), p. 6.

Which he met—it is obvious—in the terrifying posture of the
    innocent. His eyes open, proud, the whole forest moving
    still on the umblemished retina.

Nothing in the brain but a dead echo of the sky.

Only in the hollow of his left ear some light fine sand, as
    though in a shell. Which means that often he had walked
    by the sea alone with the pain of love and the roar of
    the wind.

As for those particles of fire on his groin, they show that he
    moved time hours ahead whenever he embraced a
    woman.

We shall have early fruit this year.

In this poem we are given a portrait of what the poet finds
to be most vital in his contemporary landscape through the
metaphor of a body cut open to reveal its concealed mysteries.
In the first instance, I take it to be the body of the poet that
is the subject of the autopsy, and what the probing knife
uncovers are those sources in the modern world that have best
nourished his poetic voice. But as is usual in Elytis's verse
from any period, the figure of the poet cannot be separated
from its roots in his native soil, so that we come to see the
dissected body in this poem as that of his country as well;
and what the autopsy serves to reveal is the timeless collection
of features that gives Greece what Elytis sees as her true face.
The mythical dimension emerges with the reader's growing
consciousness that this autopsy is also meant to suggest a kind
of ritual sacrifice preparing the way for perennial fertility in
keeping with ancient tradition, specifically that which offers
of the resurrected Adonis. And that is why the poem ends
with what would otherwise seem a highly enigmatic tag line
about this year's early fruit. But my commentary makes the
mythical dimension appear more blatant than the poet in-
tended it to be. As in the best of Elytis, there are mysteries
here that lie beyond explication, and that is what keeps this

poem as vital as it was when it first came out more than twenty years ago to demonstrate that Elytis's gift was still wonderfully alive after his long silence following World War II. Now that gift has earned him the Nobel Prize, and if the gods continue to look on him with favor, this late recognition abroad will serve to bring him the full international audience his work deserves.

RITSOS: VOICE AND VISION
IN THE SHORTER POEMS

The five volumes that are the focus of this essay cannot be regarded by any means as fully representative of Ritsos's shorter poems, but they do come from four different periods of his long career—the mid-forties, the fifties, the late sixties, and the mid-seventies—which permits us to consider the progress of the poet's vision over a spread of thirty years, and they are sufficiently similar in mode to encourage the view that they constitute a persistent feature of the poet's mature voice. The two earliest volumes carry the same title, *Parentheses*, the one dated 1946-1947 and the other 1950-1961.[1] A third volume, written in 1975, was chosen by the poet himself to accompany a translation of the other two,[2] presumably because he considers the poems in this relatively recent volume to be in the same general mode as the earlier "parenthetical" works. It is in any case a consideration worth exploring, because the relation of this volume and several others of the later periods to the earlier works, along with the poet's development in mode and perspective over the spread

[1] *Parentheses, 1946-47* appears in volume II of the Kedros edition of Ritsos's *Poems*. The Greek text of the selection of previously unpublished poems entitled *Parentheses, 1950-61* appeared for the first time in *Ritsos in Parentheses*, trans. and ed. Edmund Keeley (Princeton, 1979).

[2] In the *Ritsos in Parentheses* volume. The translations of poems from these three volumes quoted in this essay are from the Princeton edition.

of time these volumes encompass, allow us to place his current voice in an illuminating context that seems to have been indicated by the poet himself.[3]

In what sense are the two earliest volumes "parentheses"? They are not really an interlude between those longer works that were primarily responsible for shaping Ritsos's reputation in Greece—for example, "Epitaphios," "Romiosini," and "Moonlight Sonata"—because shorter poems of the kind found in these two volumes have been important from the beginning of the poet's career and have now come to dominate his *oeuvre*. One might call them parenthetical to those poems—early poems, on the whole—that promoted political themes directly and that helped to establish Ritsos as the leading communist poet; but to regard them as an "aside" in this sense is to give them less weight than they deserve and perhaps too much weight to the ideological aspect of Ritsos's work and to his more blatantly political, rhetorical, and sometimes loquacious exercises. In my view, some of his shorter poems reveal subtleties—the product of a tight, carefully wrought texture—that are not as available in his looser narrative and dramatic works. In any case, the voice we hear in the shorter poems, especially those written under the pressures of war and exile, and those that respond to the experience of living under the 1967-1974 dictatorship,[4] must now be seen as a major form for conveying the poet's sense of alienation both as a dispossessed Greek and as a victim of the larger spiritual crisis of our times.

To begin with the two "parentheses" volumes, I take the

[3] Ritsos did not object to this inference when he read these remarks in an early, abridged version of this essay that appeared in *Boston University Journal*, No. 3 (1978), reprinted in Greek translation in *Dedicated to Yannis Ritsos* (Athens, 1981).

[4] Ritsos was first sent into exile on the island of Limnos in 1948, then to prison camps on Makronisos in 1949 and on Ai Strati in 1950. He was released in 1952. In 1967 he was again arrested under the Papadopoulos dictatorship and sent to prison camps first on Yiaros and then on Leros. In 1968, after a month of hospitalization in Athens, he was sent into exile on the island of Samos, under house arrest at his wife's home there, and was finally allowed to return to Athens in 1970.

title of each to provide an approach to the attitudes and themes that link these earlier volumes to each other and to some of Ritsos's later work in a related mode. I am not sure what the poet himself had in mind when he chose the term, but certain metaphoric possibilities suggest themselves if "parentheses" are seen in the context of mathematics and symbolic logic, that is, as a way of designating separate groupings of symbols that form a unit or collective entity. The analogy underlines one aspect of the two volumes: a unity of symbolic vision or sensibility, both within the individual volumes and linking them to each other. Each shapes its own parenthesis enclosing a particular way of viewing reality at a particular moment in the poet's career. At the same time the two volumes, the two parentheses, are part of a developing vision that distinguishes these poems, and others related to them in terms of stance, mode, and perspective, from many works—especially the longer works—that make up Ritsos's vast *oeuvre*. The developing vision can be seen as an expansion of the space within the parenthesis representing each of the separate volumes. In the case of each, the two signs of the parenthesis are like cupped hands facing each other across a distance, hands that are straining to come together, to achieve a meeting that would serve to reaffirm human contact between isolated presences; but though there are obvious gestures toward closing the gap between the hands, the gestures seem inevitably to fail, and the meeting never quite occurs. In terms of the poet's development, the distance within the parenthesis becomes greater as we move from the first to the second volume. If we were to extend the metaphor to include the poet's late work, by the time we reach *The Distant* (the title especially significant in this context), the space between the cupped hands has become almost infinite, seemingly too vast for any ordinary human gesture that might try to bridge the parenthetical gap.

But before attempting to summarize the progress of the poet's vision, I want to consider the various volumes in chronological order, using several representative poems from each to review the particular mode and perspective that distinguish the separate stages of Ritsos's development in these shorter works. The opening poem of *Parentheses, 1946-47*, "The Meaning of Simplicity," serves to introduce several of the poet's central preoccupations:

I hide behind simple things so you'll find me;
if you don't find me, you'll find the things,
you'll touch what my hand has touched,
our hand-prints will merge.

The August moon glitters in the kitchen
like a tin-plated pot (it gets that way because of what I'm saying
    to you),
it lights up the empty house and the house's kneeling silence—
always the silence remains kneeling.

Every word is a doorway
to a meeting, one often cancelled,
and that's when a word is true; when it insists on the meeting.

The stance is that of a poet-persona who is hiding and who assumes that the reader will search to find him, will reach out to meet him and to touch if not his hand, at least his hand-print. A certain distance is taken for granted—the gap within a parenthesis, if you will—and at least the possibility of a failure to meet. But also taken for granted at this stage is the necessity of the attempt. The poem reads almost as though it were a credo: "Like Cavafy, I can be understood only from hidden things, but the things I hide behind are simple, and there is access to them through words when the words are true. Reader, try to find me through my words, because I want a meeting, no matter how difficult it may be for us to reach each other—in fact, I insist on the meeting."

This poem is one of the very few seemingly personal statements among the twenty-one that make up *Parentheses, 1946-47*. The first-person voice does not appear again until the last poem in the volume; between the first and the last we find poems that make use of the second person, the third person, first-person plural, second-person plural, any grammatical strategy for avoiding the simple "I" of lyrical or subjective statement, further evidence of the poet's impulse to hide, in this regard behind an objective stance.

The best poems in this volume are those that offer a dramatic context to supplement Ritsos's calculated—not to say programmatic—objectivity in mode of narration. The best poems are also far from simple, for all their apparent focus on relatively simple things. "Miniature" is a case in point, among the subtlest and finest of the many hundred shorter poems that Ritsos has written:

The woman stood up in front of the table. Her sad hands
    begin to cut thin slices of lemon for tea
like yellow wheels for a very small carriage
made for a child's fairy tale. The young officer sitting opposite
is buried in the old armchair. He doesn't look at her.
He lights up his cigarette. His hand holding the match trembles,
throwing light on his tender chin and the teacup's handle. The
    clock
holds its heartbeat for a moment. Something has been
    postponed.
The moment has gone. It's too late now. Let's drink our tea.
Is it possible, then, for death to come in that kind of carriage?
To pass by and go away? And only this carriage to remain,
with its little yellow wheels of lemon
parked for so many years on a side street with unlit lamps,
and then a small song, a little mist, and then nothing?

The simple things in this poem are an unidentified woman, an unidentified officer, some thin slices of lemon, an old armchair, a match, a cigarette, a teacup. And the action is really an absence of action: a visit that could lead to a meeting of some kind, a coming together that finally does not take place. Yet what a complex miniature drama it is. And those simple slices of lemon become a beautifully complicated metaphor that is the heart of the poem. The woman and the young officer face each other across their basic furniture with some expectation in their undefined relationship, enough expectation anyway to keep the visitor from looking at the woman and to make his hand tremble as it holds the match. Is it a purely erotic possibility, a potential meeting of lovers at the most fundamental level? It would hardly seem so when those simple slices of lemon that the woman's sad hands are preparing for tea shape a small carriage that invokes a distant fairy-tale world of childhood and, by extension, the mother-son aspect of this encounter between a woman of unidentified age and an officer specifically designated as young, with a "tender chin." In any case, before this ambiguous expectation of love can be realized, the clock holds its heartbeat for a moment, time is suspended, then the meeting at whatever level is postponed, and the moment of possible touching, whether physical or emotional or both, passes and is gone. And in its passing, the lemon-slice carriage of a child's fairy tale is replaced by an invisible carriage bearing death. The death of the moment's possibilities? The death of such ambiguous expectations? Or more literally, a foreshadowing of the officer's death in battle and the doom of any future for him (these poems written between 1946 and 1947 sometimes give strong hints of the larger historical context, the ruthless civil war, that the dates of their composition evoke)?

The several questions raised by the poem are beyond simple things, and the poem implies each question without offering a precise answer to any one. We know only that the carriage bearing death has come and gone in the moment of mystery when the clock stopped its heartbeat, that the expectation of more than a meeting over tea has been postponed, that it is now too late for a consummation of this trembling encounter between woman and man sometimes playing mother and son. There can be no further challenge to death now, temporary or otherwise. Their attention returns to the tea table, left now with only that lemon-wheel carriage parked on its unlit side street—its street of lost hopes and impossible expectations, perhaps—and soon not even that but the dwindling life of a song diminishing to a little mist and then to nothing.

The poem that follows "Miniature" in *Parentheses, 1946-47*, "Women," is one of the two selected from this volume for inclusion in George Veloudis's "historical" anthology of Ritsos[5]—preferred, I suppose, because the surface of it has an immediate appeal that seems to place it closer than others to what is normally regarded as the mainstream of Ritsos's verse, at least that current in it having to do with the poor and their burdens. But below the surface there are further subtle strategies and ambiguities that link this poem to the previous one and to others that show us failed gestures which are meant to establish some contact between more or less isolated people, failed attempts to break out of loneliness or aloneness and—in terms of our metaphor—to shorten the distance that separates the two cupped hands that face each other in a parenthesis:

Women are very distant. Their sheets smell of "good night."
They set the bread down on the table so that we don't
        feel they're absent.
Then we recognize that it was our fault. We get up out of the chair
        and say:
"You worked awfully hard today," or "Forget it. I'll light the lamp."

When we strike the match, she turns slowly and moves off
with inexplicable concentration toward the kitchen. Her back
is a bitterly sad hill loaded with many dead—
the family's dead, her dead, your own death.

You hear her footsteps creak on the old floorboards,
hear the dishes cry in the rack, and then you hear
the train that's taking the soldiers to the front.

The title is generic, and so is the opening: "Women are very distant." It is not "the" woman of the previous poem or of

[5] *Epitome* (Athens, 1977).

155

later poems where the definite article serves to make the term almost purely symbolic. To begin with, it is women in general who are distant, whose sheets put one off with the kind of "good night" that suggests a turning of the back—and this use of the generic term itself establishes distance, impersonality, as does the responding "we" of the second line, an attempt by the poet initially to bring us into this conspiracy of gestures, the first of which suggests rejection by "women" but which is soon followed by a gesture on their part that seems an attempt to fill the distance, the gap between "them" and "us": "they set bread on the table" so that their absence is less painful to us. And we respond with a like gesture by offering to light the lamp, because we recognize our role in the creation of this distance: "it was our fault." As we strike the match, women in general suddenly become a single, more personal "she," turning away from our gesture with a bitter burden of death on her back, including, unnervingly, "your own."

By the end of the second stanza not only has there been a grammatical movement from the general to the more personal in the woman's case, but the first-person plural identifying the general male protagonist has shifted to the second-person singular, again a grammatical gesture toward the more personal, one that now includes not only a more specific protagonist but the reader as well, the "hypocrite lecteur," if you will. Then, as the woman turns away again and moves farther into her private world of sorrow where the dishes cry in the rack, you—you, me, and the poet's persona—see that her sorrow is perhaps not so personal as we have begun to take for granted, occasioned not so much by our role in life and our failed gestures or even by the family dead and our own death that she bears as by the fate of those soldiers on their way to the front and by the woman's symbolic role as grieving lover, wife, mother to them all—what we carry to this poem from the ambiguous confrontation in the poem that precedes it. The allusion to the soldiers on their way to battle has turned the rhythm of our little drama right back to the general context from which it started and from which the poet's subtle grammatical gesturing in the second stanza seemed about to save us. Women *are* very distant in the end, and they have good reason to be, given the tragic roles we and the times force them to play. And that distance, though bridged occasionally by gestures on both their part and ours, seems as sadly inevitable and inexorable by the time we reach the last line as the poet suggested it was in the first.

My bringing into the discussion of this poem implications established in the previous one may appear arbitrary, but it is consistent with the poet's mode in these poems, which is to build a collective statement through the repetition of related motifs from one poem to another, a mode that becomes even more obvious and dramatic in its effect in Ritsos's latest collections. A few lines from other poems in the volume will illustrate the collective aspect of one central theme we have been exploring, that of the lonely or alone aspiring, and usually failing, to meet another isolated presence, and with the failure, sometimes settling for self-sufficiency. From "Maybe, Someday": "But I'm going to insist on seeing and showing you, he said, / because if you too don't see, it will be as if I hadn't— / I'll insist at least on not seeing with your eyes— / and maybe someday, from a different direction, we'll meet"; from a poem called "Self-Sufficiency?": "Under the trees two chairs. Why two? / Ah yes, one to sit on, one for stretching your legs"; from "Understanding": ". . . To be able to look / outside yourself—warmth and peacefulness. Not to be / 'only you' but 'you too' . . ."; and from "The Same Star": "That man suspects that in every mirror / there's another, transparent woman, locked in her nakedness / —much as you may want to wake her, she won't wake up. / She fell asleep smelling a star. / And he lies awake smelling that same star."

It would be hard to argue for the same kind of thematic coherence in the case of *Parentheses, 1950-61*, which is really a sampling from a larger group of unpublished poems written over a much longer period of time.[6] Yet there are related

---

[6] The selection was made by the poet himself from a manuscript notebook

preoccupations and strategies in this second volume, as the poet's choice of title emphasizes. Failure of contact and recourse to self-sufficiency are there again in one of the few first-person exercises, a rather wry little poem called "A Wreath," where the isolated persona decides to crown himself with a wreath made of the leaves that have successfully kept him from finding the person he has been trying to reach. A more insistent theme is that of our failure to cope with the realities of both civilization and nature, of our being at a loss in an environment that does not comprehend our sometimes misdirected or awkward intentions—and I say "our" because this theme is usually expressed in the first-person plural, presumably in order to establish a more general relevance and again to solicit the reader's complicity. In "Delay" we find ourselves arriving late at the theater—"we're always late"—stumbling over the knees and the insentient feet of an ugly old woman, suddenly feeling that we're the ones on stage because the lights go on and the clapping seems directed at us. And in "Message," the message has clearly not gotten through to us that nature is preparing for planting and rebirth while we go on putting in a heating stove and ignoring the obvious signs of blue skies ahead: the plumber's blue overalls, the new pipes shining like the trunks of trees, and most of all, the sturdy blue eggs that the chickens have begun to lay beside the wine barrel and the plow.

But the most persistent theme in this group focuses not on our misdirected actions that seem to go contrary to nature or on our stumbling attempts to find our place in a perverse environment but on our not being able to act at all or on our obsession with things that don't happen and places that are empty and closed. One poem is called "Inertia"; another is called "He Who Didn't Dance." And in "The Only," it isn't

---

bearing the title "Parentheses, 1950-61." At the time he made the selection he indicated that he had a large number of unpublished poems from various periods put away for possible future publication, though, he suggested, since he was already accused of being too prolific, he wasn't in any hurry to reveal how much he still had hidden away in manuscript form.

enough that what has been anticipated for some time doesn't in fact happen—the "what" never even identified—but those who have anticipated something happening find, as they take the flags down, that they are left with only one prop to sustain them in place of action, only one substitute for the once expected but now missing barbarian solution in this neo-Cavafian world: the lack of any excuse. In the same poem we learn that "the walls smell strongly of unfamiliarity," as well they might in such alienated circumstances. At other times in *Parentheses, 1950-61*, the surroundings smell of emptiness, of absence, of the wrong season, because, as "Autumn Expression" puts it, "The great dampness has set in. The vacationers have left." From "Desk Calendar" we learn that "everyone has gone abroad" in midwinter, leaving us with "Desperate gestures by the wind / in front of the closed hotel's glass door."

Ritsos doesn't designate precise sources or reasons for the sense of dislocation and absence, of inertia and silence, that pervade the landscape he paints in this second volume of "parentheses" poems, nor does he offer clear indication of what might bring about a change in his country of suspended possibilities and aborted expectations—a stance here and elsewhere that gives the lie to his being simply a propagandist for extreme political solutions, as he was sometimes accused of being by the Greek literary establishment during the fifties (when he was acknowledged at all). The only clue we have to his vision of the future, of the way things may turn, in this admittedly incomplete image of his perspective during the decade emerges from two of the more substantial and complicated poems in *Parentheses, 1950-61*, both of which suggest the possible advent of new gods to replace the old—and a new attitude toward gods however defined—in Ritsos's contemporary landscape. The first, "In the Ruins of an Ancient Temple," places the old and the new in direct juxtaposition:

The museum guard was smoking in front of the sheepfold.
The sheep were grazing among the marble ruins.
Farther down the women were washing in the river.

You could hear the beat of the hammer in the blacksmith's
    shop.
The shepherd whistled. The sheep ran to him
as though the marble ruins were running. The water's thick
    nape
shone with coolness behind the oleanders. A woman
spread her washed clothing on the shrubs and the statues—
she spread her husband's underpants on Hera's shoulders.

Foreign, peaceful, silent intimacy—years on years. Down on the
    shore
the fishermen passed by with broad baskets full of fish
on their heads, as though they were carrying long and narrow
    flashes of light:
gold, rose, and violet—the same as that procession bearing
the long richly embroidered veil of the goddess that we cut up
    the other day
to arrange as curtains and tablecloths in our emptied houses.

One might be tempted to see the poem as simply an ironic
treatment of the relation between antiquity and a modern
sensibility, a kind of mock pastoral say: the shepherd and
even the guard seem to accept the ancient marble ruins as
ordinary, everyday objects in their bucolic landscape, as though
the ruins have been drained by time of any godly association
whatsoever and are now as much a part of this world as the
very earthly sheep gamboling among them—in fact, at one
point sheep and ruins cannot be distinguished from each other:
". . . The sheep ran to him / as though the marble ruins were
running." And the woman with her washing, of the first stanza—
I suppose the best that we can get for a nymph in this modern
landscape—is wonderfully casual toward the ancient gods,
not to say downright sacrilegious, in hanging her husband's
underpants on Hera's shoulders. Also, in the second stanza,
in place of the old procession honoring a goddess, we have
fishermen with baskets full of flashing, multicolored fish—

even worse, the goddess's richly embroidered veil has been cut up to make curtains and tablecloths.

But is it really worse? Is the poet's stance ironic? The poem seems to offer a contrary, anyway an ambivalent, implication: there may be good reason for these new primitives to submit to practical necessity when the old gods have lost their godly relevance and when the houses people are supposed to live in have been emptied. Rather than simple irony, one gets the sense of territory being cleared—or more to the point, of air being cleared—for new beginnings. In treating the ancient gods so casually, with such familiarity, in turning them from agents of mystery into useful domestic objects as necessity demands, these inhabitants of a modern pastoral world seem not only to have accommodated their ancient past but to have neutralized it, as though preparing for new gods, as though preparing perhaps to start the divine cycle over again in terms of the contemporary reality they actually live, even if their new or redefined gods prove less marble-constant and accessible.

This interpretation would appear to gain some support from the second poem specifically having to do with gods, "Incense," in particular the concluding lines, where lighting up a cigarette is seen as a new kind of divine ritual (we may have been prepared for this by the persistent smoking in Ritsos's poems, as in his workshop) and where cigarette smoke—joining that from the houses with some rooms still closed—becomes the new incense:

He gazed at the morning through the windowpanes. He felt
    with precision
that the blue rolls along the bird's skin or the cloud's.
He suspected that the same sense of touch was at the tree's
    disposal also.
The smoke emerged from the chimneys as though confessing
    the secret
of heat in the rooms that were still closed.

In this way, every morning, all the houses smoke.
And the men, emerging early for work,
light up their cigarettes while still on the threshold, as though
    remembering
some unknown, unapproachable deity entirely their own.

What is the god now honored in this poem, at least in
memory? One unknown, unapproachable, designated as "en-
tirely their own" (to distinguish him, presumably, from gods
belonging to others, to the old tradition, to enemies, whoever
they may be exactly)—a god otherwise unnamed and unde-
fined. That this god is acknowledged on the threshold of par-
tially closed space and that he is unapproachable does not
come as a surprise, given the themes we have already en-
countered in this volume of poems. At the same time, it *is* on
a threshold that the men seem to remember him, and they are
in the process of emerging from the closed, glassed-in quarters
of the first stanza into the open air on their way to work,
suggesting, perhaps, that it is a new hearth-god their smoke
has signaled. That is as much as the poem offers in the way
of a prospect for the future, and given both the god's attributes
and the merely hypothetical evocation of him, it is an equiv-
ocal prospect at best.

When we arrive at the poems of the Junta years (1967-
1974), the equivocation is replaced by almost total disloca-
tion, in both spiritual and physical terms: a dramatic disrup-
tion of the imagery representing the Greek tradition in myth
and religion, all sense of place transformed into a sense of
exile, dispossession, constant relocation, and self-sufficiency
now reduced to self-alienation. There are a number of volumes
of shorter poems that one might draw on for a characteri-
zation of the rich if harsh vision of these years. I will concen-
trate on three groups of poems from different phases of the
poet's experience under the dictatorship in order to illustrate
the progress of his vision under the pressure of that particular
history, the first a group of some fifty-six poems that the poet
wrote between November 1967 and January 1968—i.e., dur-

ing the first year after the military takeover, while he was incarcerated at the "Concentration Camp for Political Detainees, Partheni, Leros"—and that make up half the volume entitled *The Wall Inside the Mirror* (the other half of the volume, which will not concern us here, covers the period March-October, 1971).[7] A second group, from the volume called *Muted Poems*, was written in 1972, two years before the collapse of the dictatorship (and has yet to appear in Greek).[8] The third volume, *The Distant*, was written a year after the regime fell, and was published in 1977.

The 1967-1968 poems from *The Wall Inside the Mirror* offer a landscape that seems to contain some of the expected elements that characterize the Greek landscape, even in Ritsos's earlier verse—poor fields, stones, olive trees, vineyards, plows, farm animals—but here the image is subject to sudden, violent distortion and to the intrusion of anomalies (I will quote generously from this volume and from the one that will engage us next, because most of the relevant poems are not yet readily available in English translation):[9]

[7] The poems in this volume were first published in a French translation by Dominique Grandmont (without the Greek text) in 1973 under the Gallimard imprint. The first Greek edition, by Kedros, appeared in Athens in November of 1974, one of Ritsos's early publications in Greece after the collapse of the dictatorship. In the French edition (which includes most, but not all, of the poems that appear in the Greek edition), each poem is dated. It is clear from these dates that two periods of creative work are included in the volume, one from November 1967 to January 1968 on Leros and one from March to October of 1971 in Athens, Corinth, Delphi, and the island of Samos. The phrase "Concentration Camp for Political Detainees / PARTHENI LEROS / November 1967-January 1968" appears at the foot of the poem "Return" on p. 63 of the Greek edition, and it is followed by a poem ("For No Reason") that the French edition dates "21.iii.71."

[8] The English translations offered here are by the author and first appeared in *Chelsea*, No. 40 (Winter, 1981), pp. 38-45.

[9] The translations offered here are by the author. For additional translations into English, see Yannis Ritsos, *The Fourth Dimension*, trans. Rae Dalven (Boston, 1977), pp. 151-156; Yannis Ritsos, *Chronicle of Exile*, trans. Minas Savvas (San Francisco, 1977), pp. 44-45; and Andonis Decavalles, trans., "From *The Wall in the Mirror*: Eleven Poems," *The Falcon*, No. 16 (Spring, 1978), pp. 32-41.

OUR LAND

We climbed the hill to look over our land:
fields poor and few, stones, olive trees.
Vineyards head toward the sea. Beside the plow
a small fire smoulders. We shaped the old man's clothes
into a scarecrow against the ravens. Our days
are making their way toward a little bread and great sunshine.
Under the poplars a straw hat beams.
The rooster on the fence. The cow in yellow.
How did we manage to put our house and our life in order
with a hand made of stone? Up on the lintel
there's soot from the Easter candles, year by year:
tiny black crosses marked there by the dead
returning from the Resurrection Service. This land is much loved
with patience and dignity. Every night, out of the dry well,
the statues emerge cautiously and climb the trees.

One doesn't have to see those ravens as an echo of Achma-
tova's ravens of death to sense that this much-loved landscape
is threatened by a deadly evil:[10] the people in it have turned
to stone, and the statues into cautious people climbing the
trees. Even more ominous, instead of the living who have been
given new life at the Easter Eve Service by the resurrected
Christ, we learn that it is the dead who have returned home
with their lighted candles to mark the lintel with the tradi-
tional cross of soot.[11]

Several poems in the group extend the sense of dislocated

[10] See Poem No. 16, from *Wayside Herb*, 1921. The concluding lines of
the poem are rendered by Tom Alderson (in manuscript) as follows:

> To the west the light still hangs in the sky
> And the roofs of the cities shimmer in the sun.
> But here they've already marked the houses with a cross;
> They've called the ravens, the ravens are flying.

[11] The cross so marked is meant to carry the implications of the Resurrec-
tion Service through the year following, when a new cross is again marked
on the lintel.

tradition within the Christian context. In "Inexplicable Times," we are told that "in those days everything was strange," so much so that the monks left the monasteries to become peddlers, to climb trees in their robes, catch owls, cook them behind the cemetery wall. In "Continued Waiting," those waiting for the messenger near a long-forgotten table by a path that is "all stones and thorns" are finally greeted by the supervisor who sets twelve glasses on the table; but since one of the glasses falls off and breaks, these dispossessed disciples have to start waiting from the beginning again. The failure of the Greek tradition to provide the spiritual resources that might restore life to this dying landscape includes the ancient phases of that tradition. In *Parentheses, 1950-61*, the procession bearing the veil of the goddess, that which had been cut up to make curtains, was compared to the passing of fishermen carrying baskets of multicolored fish on their heads ("In the Ruins of an Ancient Temple"), what we took to be at best an accommodation, and at worst a neutralization, of ancient tradition. Here, in "Evening Procession," those taking part in the procession have undergone a metamorphosis that has more terrifying implications:

Poor soil, very poor; burnt shrubs, stones—
we loved these stones, we worked them. Time goes by,
brilliant sunsets. A mauve glow on the windows.
Behind the windows earthen pots, unmarried girls.
Mists come up from the olive grove. When evening falls,
the procession of those wearing veils starts up from the
    cypress trees;
their gait, somehow rigid, has a sad, archaic dignity;
you can tell suddenly from the gait that their knees
are marble, broken, stuck back together with cement.

The mutilation and destruction of ancient tradition under the pressure of a catastrophic, dehumanizing current history is overtly represented in two poems that make use of the Trojan horse as a central symbol. In the first, "Transgression," we find the ever-present "he" opening a kitchen door to spot three hunters "burning / the wooden horse in the oven"—all except its eyes, which won't burn. The "he" closes the door silently and goes out into the garden. In "Exploration," the "he" hears the wooden horse squeaking in the garden and finds it opening its left flank to let out "the twelve wounded swordsmen." He manages to lock these symbols of a later tradition inside the house and returns to take over the horse, locking himself inside so that he can smoke a cigarette and watch the smoke emerge from the horse's eyes.

The poet is not coy about the most immediate causes of this pervasive dislocation. Though, in keeping with his late mode, the context is never overtly political, and though the implications of any given text are not restricted to their political reference, indications of an immediate source in the actions of the dictatorial regime are inescapable even if the poetic resonance of the text depends on a symbolic extension of specific events to the human predicament more generally. "Change of Habits" clearly emerges from the experience of those called to account by the Junta and sent into exile during the early days of the military takeover, though the response to these events is given an imaginative ironic twist, a touch of the grotesque, typical of Ritsos's rendering of the human effort to survive under extreme external threat:

In front of the door they read a list. Those
who heard their names got ready in a hurry—
a torn suitcase, a bundle, the rest left behind.
The place emptied steadily, shrunk. Those who
    remained gathered in tightly.
With a certain reticence and solemnity they set up a forgotten
    alarm clock
in the far corner of the room. From then on, every night,
each taking his turn, they wound it, waiting serenely for it to
    go off
at 6:15 the next morning so that they could go out and wash.
    One day

it went off at midnight. They got up, washed—the moon was
    out—
then sat around the alarm clock to smoke a cigarette.

In several poems the setting is identified as a camp of some
kind, with those inside under constant surveillance (guards
and a canteen are actually indicated in "After Rain"), subject
to threat and intimidation by mysterious, unidentified figures.
In "Limits," for example, a bugle sounds well past midnight.
People look out of their windows, then hide behind drawn
curtains. Only "the man in charge of water" goes out with
his dog baying at the moon. Then five masked men appear,
undress completely in the communal bathroom, but don't
remove their masks. The pressure of not knowing what is
likely to happen next, of where one is likely to be sent, leads
to constant directionless motion and aimless efforts to fill
empty space, a drastic extension of the metaphor of emptiness
seen in *Parentheses, 1950-61*: "We couldn't stand what was
empty, uninhabited. Often we would move / the huge mirror
to the river bank, a chair / onto a tree; and at other times,
conversely, / a huge tree into the dining room." And in "Priv-
ilege," the sense of dislocation, of unwilled motion, finds mo-
mentary relief only in the motionless window and wall inside
a mirror:

This up and down, he says, I don't understand it.
To forget myself I look into the small mirror;
I see the motionless window, I see the wall—
nothing changes inside or outside the mirror.
I leave a flower on the chair (for as long as it lasts).
I live here, at this number, on this street.
And suddenly they raise me (the chair and the flower too),
they lower me, raise me—I don't know. Luckily
I managed to put this mirror in my pocket.

The alienation in these poems appears to reach the point
where one turns in on oneself not out of the hope for survival

on self-sufficient resources but out of the sleepless need to confirm that one exists, usually with the help of a mirror: "Late in the evening, around eight, when the stores close, the mirrors / empty all at once. Everyone—clerk or owner or customers— / takes a mirror and shuts himself up in his room, / while in the streets outside the stillness of insomnia already begins to jell." The "he" finally becomes a wax image of himself, yet even so, naked among real wax images, a woman comes along and points him out, saying: "This one seems less natural." And in "Elation," his self-alienation becomes so complete that he can apparently—perhaps with a touch of irony—stand outside himself and take pleasure in the purity of his foreignness:

> the way things have gone empty little by little,
> there's nothing left for him to do. He sits alone,
> looks at his hands, his fingernails—they're foreign—
> he touches his chin again and again, notices
> another chin, so simply foreign,
> so deeply and naturally foreign that even he himself
> begins to take pleasure in its novelty.

In a world so dislocated and alienated, simple things take on new significance: they become the last link to a tangible reality, to the way things were—"melancholy things" in "Elegy," such as "a letter-opener, comb, matches, a cigarette / smoking itself in the ashtray," or, in "Untitled Events," things remembered from elsewhere, as distant as an odor of cologne that can't adjust itself to exile:

Memory didn't meet things. Events
were left without room, they dissolved. Of course you could
imagine an ashtray elsewhere, a clothes-hanger,
the odor of cologne from some neighborhood barbershop
a little before the stores close Saturday evening—
even the lovely woman who dallied to scratch a tangerine
vanished late at night in the Station's glare, smelling her fingers—

distant, distant, exiled, not even adjusting
to the chaotic ammunition chamber with its nylon curtains.

The poem that concludes this 1967-68 section of *The Wall
Inside the Mirror* is the only one in the Greek edition that is
dated, and the date offered is a summary one ("November
1967-January 1968") presumably meant to cover the whole
section. From the French edition of these poems, the first
edition,[12] we learn that the poem was actually written in No-
vember of 1968, which suggests that it is the product of some
reflection of the poet's experience as a "detainee" at the Par-
theni, Leros, Camp. It has the aura of a defining image, one
that shows us the city cleared first of statues, then of nature
and people. The city is left to its own desolate devices. Finally
one man returns to plant his key in the ground, then the
statues. It is not an image with much hope in it, but it may
suggest the first desperate gestures toward reversal, and it does
carry the title "Return":

> The statues left first. A little later
> the trees, people, animals. The land
> became entirely desert. The wind blew.
> Newspapers and thorns circled in the streets.
> At dusk the lights went on by themselves.
> A man came back alone, looked around him,
> took out his key, stuck it in the ground
> as though planting a tree. Then he climbed
> the marble stairs and gazed down at the city.
> Carefully, one by one, the statues returned.

Four years later, in the 1972 volume *Muted Poems*, Ritsos's
landscape has become a degree more muted in its terror (in
keeping with one implication of the volume's title), but those
who inhabit it are still physically and spiritually dispossessed,
and their accommodation to a repressive history has muted

---

[12] See n. 7 above.

them in costly ways (the dictatorship was preparing a rigged election of its leader to the presidency at this time, a year before Papadopoulos was deposed and Ioannides assumed power for his brief and disastrous term as Junta dictator). The people have returned to the city, and the statues are still alive—"look[ing] in front of them quietly, purely, not at all accusingly"—but the city's inhabitants are generally crippled and old: blind men, old unmarried women, beggars, crones, a man with his right hand always in his pocket clutching his identity card, a woman wearing a yellow mask and another with her face eaten away. This physical disintegration is the outward sign of an inner crippling that has left the inhabitants with a moral and intellectual lethargy that engenders indecision, inaction, indifference. In "Sad Cunning," the poem's "he" is overcome by "that sense out of the absence of sensation . . . the untried lethargy":

should he change position, light the lamp, or stay down there
in the hypothetical wheelchair, from which he extends
his left hand to touch the iron rim of one wheel
as though grasping the helm of an ancient, distant power,
tired and indifferent, not out to command anyone?

In "Out of Place," people are seen to "remain motionless, almost sad; they can't get angry any longer; they can't feel sorry for the others any longer." And in "Compulsory Assent," it is no longer clear whether the people or their tormentors are most overcome by the general lethargy; in any case, there seems to be a complicity not to see too much on the part of both (the "they" here carries that ambiguity at times), a sharing in compulsory discretion as well as assent:

Who bared the windows like that, the doors, the trees, the stones?
They stay back out of the way, discreet, pretending not to see;
they actually don't see; they let the hanged man free to swing on
    his rope,

the soldier to piss in the sheepfold; the woman with her single
    earring;
the crone with her basket of eggs. . . .

In this community of the muted, the unseeing, the indiffer-
ent, life appears to have become a bad game of charades in
which posture and gesture take the place of forceful stance
and action, and the most representative figures in the land-
scape are players without a legitimate theater. In "Out of
Place," we learn that "Their stage sets and wardrobes had
been seized. Now / what costumes are they to play in, without
red stage curtains and cardboard forests, / without the lion's
gate . . . ?" The player in "Among the Blind" not only finds
himself performing without success before an audience of the
blind but sees that they too are playing their own game of
charades:

What more could he do, circulating day and night
among the ten blind men. He tried
invisible postures, indecipherable gestures—sometimes
completely naked, sometimes wearing the shirt and sword
of dead heroes, sometimes wearing the transparent dress
of the lost mythical woman; and the changes
always convincing, without need of proof. The blind men
ate a lot, slept well. . . . And he himself,
he knew perfectly well that the blind were not at all blind.

We discover from "The End of the Performance" that the
reason the old women wearing the masks of the blind have
become mute ("Don't ask them anything. They don't an-
swer.") is their recognition that "the time has come when
lying is no longer tolerable," and this recognition includes the
ultimate source of the spiritual tranquility they once knew:
"that handsome, polite, that most innocent liar in the world,
/ the one with the wide sleeves for hiding his bound hands."
Even more blatantly than in the previous volume, the poet
pictures the country's traditional spiritual resources as having

dried up, victim of the same crippling alienation that infects the communal life in general, whether those resources are Christian or more ancient. In "Fellow Diners" we find that the table for the Last Supper, though set, is not for those who still have wings:

Endless transfers, unwanted or willed
and suddenly time delays, holds back;
the dead disappear; those present: absent.
the table is set. Nothing's wrong. Come in.
The twelve glasses. And one more. Still, be careful,
don't step on the floor—there is no floor. Here
those who can sit comfortably are only those
who have eaten both of their wings and are no longer hungry.

The one recourse that seems to be left for those so thoroughly incapable of believing in either a past or a future, of taking any action or position in the world of real events—those described in "Nor This" as jumping "from one thing to its opposite" or staying "in the middle, a little below or a little above"—the one recourse is some sort of artistic or symbolic representation of the life that has been lost, and this patiently carved on "a bared kernel of rice." It is a dubious representation, hardly one that brings new hope; at best it offers an image of a futile, if perhaps heroic, gesture of nostalgic recovery and mad resistance, and if one takes it for a caricature of the artist as poet,[13] it is colored by a painful self-irony: the carving consists of "a multitude of war scenes, heroes, dead men, flags, / and that beautiful, crazy deserter who, naked in front of the gun barrels, / endlessly drums away on his empty canteen."

By the time we reach *The Distant*, written some three years after the volume we have been considering, Ritsos's landscape

[13] Incidentally, though Ritsos himself is not known for carving images in any form, he has done a vast number of ink drawings (often on the backs of cigarette boxes of the kind still available in Greece) and on stones gathered up from the beach.

has taken on a consistent harshness and a bleakness equal to the most extreme characterization in the earlier works, yet there is new power in the way this latest phase of his vision is projected. The reigning deity has become, as the title poem suggests, the embodiment of distance, silence, the unapproachable, inaction—all that the earlier work pointed toward but that has now arrived at an ultimate formulation. Though the title poem is the last in the volume, it has the tone of an invocation, anyway a prayer to a god who has for some years hovered in the wings of the world created by Ritsos's shorter poems and who is here brought onto center stage to be openly hymned:

O distant, distant; deep unapproachable; receive always
the silent ones in their absence, in the absence of the others
when the danger from the near ones, from the near itself, burdens
during nights of promise with many-colored lights in the gardens,
when the half-closed eyes of lions and tigers scintillate
with flashing green omissions in their cages
and the old jester in front of the dark mirror
washes off his painted tears so that he can weep—
O quiet ungrantable, you with the long, damp hand,
quiet invisible, without borrowing and lending, without obligations,
nailing nails on the air, shoring up the world
in that deep inaction where music reigns.

The gap separating the two hands of our metaphorical parenthesis seems to have widened almost to infinity if the most tangible danger is that from "the near ones, from the near itself," and if that which serves to shore up the world is a thing that cannot be granted, a thing without obligations, living invisibly in the realm of inaction where music reigns. One might be tempted to see the reference to music as a positive sign, evidence of a saving lyrical transcendence in this country of bleak absolutes dominated by distance, silence, and the unapproachable; but the concrete "things" and characters that make up the down-to-earth landscape of these poems allow only the smallest space for this possibility of relief, at least as my eye sees the poetic territory that Ritsos shows us in this volume, after seven years of cruel history on both a national and personal level, including the poet's second period of imprisonment and exile.

Most of the elements that build the new landscape in *The Distant* are familiar from earlier poems, but they are presented in this volume in a style that has been purified of all decoration and that finds its strength in a renewed commitment to simplicity and economy (to paraphrase George Seferis's parallel ambition): no overt sentiment, no obvious metaphors, the syntax basic, the colors primary—if sometimes perverse—the details focused with precision to create a startling image of a country haunted by secret violence:

The deep voice was heard in the deeper night.
Then the tanks went by. Then day broke.
Then the voice was heard again, shorter, farther in.
The wall was white. The bread red. The ladder
rested almost vertical against the antique lamppost. The old
    woman
collected the black stones one by one in a paper bag.

The action in this poem, called "Toward Saturday," is also treated with economy, just the bare facts and no commentary: a deep voice in the night, tanks going by, an old woman collecting stones (in contrast, one assumes, to gathering wood for warmth or wild greens for food—but the poet doesn't say so). It is a powerfully rendered landscape of bad dreams, of remembered horror, with dangers and threats that remain unresolved but that are no less real for it. And if it evokes nightmares occasioned by the 1967-1974 dictatorship or earlier harsh history in Greece, it does not need that kind of local, topical definition to engender a strong response, because the images here reach more broadly into the shared psychic consciousness of our times.

Perhaps the central figure in this nightmare landscape is a

trapped victim trying to hide from unexplained forces, enemies identified only as "they" and "them": "He heard them calling his name over the water. / He verified that it was for him. He hid." (from "Secretly"). And when the unidentified "they" dig the victim out of hiding, as they surely must, they mock those gestures by him that establish his humanity:

RED-HANDED

Throw the spotlight right on his face;
hidden like this in the night, let's see him, make him glow;
he has beautiful teeth—and he knows it; he smiles
with the small moon up on the bombed-out hill,
with children of the woodcutters down by the river.

The threat of arrest and annihilation pursues the nightmare victim even in those moments that should be exhilarating, joyous, as in "Preparing the Ceremony," where the persona, about to be celebrated at a public gathering in a large hall, not only finds that he's suddenly missing but also realizes that if he were somehow to rediscover himself and get his feet to move, the usher would arrest him.

The victim's loss of contact with himself is paralleled by a total loss of contact with others in those poems that pick up the theme of two people confronting each other in some attempt at dialogue. The essential dialogue has now moved farther away from a meeting through words, as the title of one poem, "Brief Dialogue," underlines, and even the bed where it is conducted is seen by the woman in the same poem as "a silent fierce animal getting ready to leave." The distance separating the "he" and "she" in this volume appears unbridgeable. They are dead to each other—literally so, it would seem, in "Completeness Almost," even if their dialogue strives to deny it: "You know, death doesn't exist, he said to her. / I know, yes, now that I'm dead, she answered." At best they confront each other as suspicious cripples, seeing one another in the reflection from a glass eye, again literally:

COURT EXHIBIT

The woman was still lying on the bed. He
took out his glass eye, set it down on the table,
took a step, stopped. Now do you believe me? he said to her.
She picked up the glass eye, brought it close to her eye; she
    looked at him.

That final look is the one touch of ambiguity the poet allows
himself, though the general context of these poems leads us
to suspect that the "exhibit" does not really convince the lady
in the end.

    The one poem that actually offers an image of physical
contact, the three handsome young men linked shoulder to
shoulder in "Winter Sunshine," tells us, parenthetically, that
the one in the middle is a statue; and the three are seen to be
strolling "in the sunlit insouciance of death." The theme, the
death of meetings once assumed possible and necessary, finds
its logical conclusion in "With the Unapproachable," where
the "he" makes what seems an ultimate commitment of self-
sufficiency: "So very very distant—and therefore invulnerable
too—he said; / yet no one distant enough; no one as much as
he would like, / as much maybe as he could be or should be."

    The perspective of these poems—unsentimental, at times
almost dehumanized, at times dryly harsh, yet in touch with
a felt reality—emerges in its boldest outlines if we read the
poems in sequence, because here, as in the earlier volumes,
the poems build on each other to shape a composite statement,
one that is even more coherent and unified, if also at times
more disturbing, than those of the two *Parentheses*, one that
is also characteristic in its density and mode of the two other
late Ritsos volumes discussed here. The interconnected atti-
tudes, characters, and objects in *The Distant* create the kind
of general image a poetic novella might offer, though without
a plot and without transitions to bind the structure together.
The binding is the poet's relentless vision. And the reappear-
ance of persistent motifs works to establish a symbolic land-

scape that gradually becomes familiar. The elements taken by themselves may sometimes seem obscurely personal—what do the old woman's black stones represent exactly, or the recurring statues, the mirrors, the walls, the bread, etc.?—but on reading the volume through, and especially on rereading the volume through, these individual "things" begin to fall into a context, until we see them as thoroughly at home, as inevitable, in the strange new wasteland world the poet has constructed.

It is a world inhabited again on the whole by people who are old or crippled or dead, both figuratively and literally—the one-eyed, the one-armed, the petrified, the missing, those on the way to burial—a world in which nature has been drained of normal sustenance. Yet a struggle to survive, whether by hiding or by establishing a protective distance or by trying out new rituals, appears to begin again in at least some measure among these victims of undefined enemies. In "Reconstruction" (as positive a title as one is likely to find in late Ritsos) some of the individual symbols come together with unusual force to shape an especially arid image of the poet's imagined country, territory where there is no earth, where no grass grows, only stones, rafters, a burnt tree, and the burden of death again. Yet we find in the same poem a new, unexpected ritual that seems meant to rejuvenate the landscape and to reaffirm some possibility of contact between the tortured inhabitants of Ritsos's wasteland, a ritual that brings the inhabitants again in touch with the earth, the soil, as well as with each other (significantly, shoeless feet replace hands as the agents of this new attempt at a meeting) and the ends—very much in the Greek tradition—with a dance:

Then we lit the great fires; we set the old man on the rock;
we took off our boots; and sitting like this on the ground
two by two we measured our feet, soles against soles.
Young Konstandis, who had the largest feet, danced first.

The poet's thirty-year journey from *Parentheses, 1946-47*

177

to *The Distant* has been one of bitter catharsis, a progress from his focus on so-called simple things and more or less abortive gestures to a focus on bare—not to say barren—essentials and primitive rituals performed by those whose deity appears to be an infinitely distant, absolutely white, unapproachable and silent ambiguity. The starkness of this late vision, with its desiccated landscape and haunting presence of death, is paralleled by an aesthetic absoluteness that replaces the earlier grammatical complexity with an uncomplicated syntax consisting largely of declarative sentences and a purified style that leaves no room for figures of speech, no coloring other than basic adjectives, no images that have not been drained of overt sentiment. It has been a movement from masked simplicity to an attempt at the real thing. The earlier mode produced poems of subtlety and warmth, and it also produced poems marred by sentimentality; the later mode precludes sentimentality, but it does not always preclude an excess of stylistic dryness and a degree of obscurity. Yet the effect of the long catharsis in those late poems that work well is to provide a sense of reality that transcends the merely representational, a sense of the deeper psychic meanings—the hidden threats and nightmare memories—that lie below the surface of things. The poet's development has served to promote symbolic richness at the expense of decorative coloring and tragic vision at the expense of ideological rhetoric.

The development starts much earlier than has been generally acknowledged in Greek literary circles—as we have seen, at least as early as the best of *Parentheses, 1946-47*. Beginning with that volume, Ritsos appears to have moved in much the same direction as that chosen by his eminent predecessors in this century, Cavafy, Sikelianos, and Seferis. Each abandoned rhetorical self-indulgence or subjective lyricism at some point in his career in favor of the dramatic and symbolic expression of a tragic sense of life that came to each with a mature vision of the human predicament and that discovered its profoundest form in the kind of simplicity which emerges from catharsis, personal and stylistic. The five volumes of shorter poems that we have explored here can be taken as testimony of both the pain and the wisdom of Ritsos's progress toward a like discovery.

POSTSCRIPT:
A CONVERSATION
WITH SEFERIS

Seferis was nearing the end of his longest visit to the United States at the time of this interview, which took place in late December of 1968. He had just completed a three-month term as fellow of the Institute for Advanced Study in Princeton, and he was in particularly good spirits because he felt that his visit had served for a kind of rejuvenation: an interlude free from the political tensions that had been building up for some months in Athens and the occasion for both reflection and performance. The latter included a series of readings—at Harvard, Princeton, Rutgers, Pittsburgh, Washington, D.C., and the Y.M.H.A. Poetry Center in New York— Seferis reading in Greek and the interviewer in English, each appearance with its distinct qualities of excitement and response. In Pittsburgh, for example, the audience (composed mostly of local Greek-Americans) seemed bewildered by the poetry during the reading but responded to the poet during the reception afterwards as they might have to Greece's then exiled king. The New York reading began with an introduction by Senator Eugene McCarthy. During the discussion period several questions from the audience had to do specifically with the political situation in Greece. Seferis refused to answer them. He was thought to be evasive by some in the audience, but he held his ground, and during the dinner following the reading he gave his reasons in private: he didn't consider it proper to criticize his government while a guest on foreign soil, safe from the consequences of the government's displeasure. He saved his answers for his return to Greece: an uncompromising statement against the dictatorship presented to local and foreign correspondents in defiance of martial law and at obvious personal risk (*The New York Times*, March 29, 1969).

The combination of diplomatic tact and high conscience that defined the political character of Seferis also colored his presence and personal style. He was a heavy man, his voice gentle when disengaged, his movements slow, almost lethargic at times; yet he had a habit of gripping your arm as he moved, and the grip, though amiable in the old-fashioned European manner, remained young and firm enough to give you word of the strength still in him. And the voice had a second edge that cut sharply when he sensed something dubious or facile challenging it. Then, on the diplomatic side again, came a sense of humor: a love of nonsense, of the risqué joke, of kidding himself and others with a wry little moon of a smile that appeared unexpectedly in his oval face—especially after he had trapped his listener with the question: "Why are you laughing?" The poet Richard Howard once referred to Seferis as a "Middle Eastern troglodyte" in a poem about his first reading in New York some years ago. When the interviewer finally got up the courage to show Seferis the poem, the Greek poet fixed him with a sharp, uncompromising look. "Middle Eastern troglodyte. Ridiculous and inaccurate. I once called myself a Cappadocian troglodyte and that is what I plan to remain. Why are you laughing?" Then the smile.

The interview took place in the Seferises' temporary home at the Institute for Advanced Study, an unpretentious second-floor apartment with three rooms, with a large window overlooking the grounds, the bookcase almost empty, none of the modern Greek paintings and classical treasures that set the style of the Seferis home in Athens. Yet the poet was delighted with the place because it gave him access to a number of apparently exotic things: changing trees, and squirrels, and children crossing the lawn from school. His wife Maro—hair still gold and braided like a girl's—was present throughout the interview, sometimes listening with evident amusement, sometimes preparing food or drinks in the background. There were three recording sessions conducted in English. Seferis would take a while to warm up with the microphone watching him from the coffee table, but whenever he began to reminisce about friends from the war years and before—Henry Miller, Durrell, Katsimbalis—or the years of his childhood, he would relax into his natural style and talk easily until the tape died out on him.

KEELEY

Let me start by asking you about the Institute for Advanced Study and how you feel, only recently retired from the diplomatic service, about beginning a new career as a student.

SEFERIS

My dear, the problem which puzzles me is: what is advanced study? Should one try to forget, or to learn more, when one is at my stage of advanced study? Now I must say, on a more prosaic level, that I enjoy very much the whole situation here because there are very nice people, very good friends and I enjoy—how shall I put it?—their horizons. There are many horizons around me: science, history, archaeology, theology, philosophy . . .

KEELEY

But don't you feel out of place among so many scientists? So many historians?

SEFERIS

No, because I am attracted by people whose interests are not in my own area.

KEELEY

Do you think there's an advantage—as I think Cavafy would probably have thought—to being in dialogue with historians? In other words, do you feel that history has something particular to say to the poet?

SEFERIS

If you remember, Cavafy was *proud* of having a sense of history. He used to say: "I am a man of history"—something like that, I don't remember the exact quotation. I am not that way; but still, I feel the pressure of history. In another way perhaps: more mythological, more abstract or more concrete . . . I don't know.

KEELEY

How about the relation of the Greek poet to his particular historical tradition? You once said that there is no ancient Greece in Greece. What did you mean by that exactly?

SEFERIS

I meant Greece is a continuous process. In English the expression "ancient Greece" includes the meaning of "finished," whereas for us Greece goes on living for better or for worse; it is *in* life, has not expired yet. That is a fact. One can make the same argument when one discusses the pronunciation of ancient Greek. Your scholars in America or in England or in France may be quite right in adopting the Erasmic pronunciation: for them Greek is a dead language; but for us it is another story. The fact is, you consider that ancient Greek has terminated its function at a certain point and this enables you to pronounce it—with my regrets—in an arbitrary way.

KEELEY

Then obviously you see the Greek tradition in language, as well as in other things, as a continuous process. That is not

183

the belief of some classical and Byzantine scholars in this country—and, I suppose, elsewhere.

SEFERIS

You know why that happens? Because the subject, the history of Greece, is so large that each scholar limits himself to a certain period or branch and nothing exists outside of it. For example, Gibbon considered that a thousand years of life were a decline. How can a people be in decline for a thousand years? After all, between the Homeric poems and the birth of Christ eight hundred years elapsed—or something like that—and then presumably there were a thousand years of decline.

KEELEY

On the question of the Greek poet's relation to his tradition, it has always seemed to me that the Greek poet has an advantage over his Anglo-Saxon counterpart who makes use of Greek mythology, and sometimes even of Greek landscape. I remember years ago when I was writing a dissertation on what I thought were English influences in the poetry of Cavafy and Seferis, I asked you about certain images that crop up in your landscape, for example the symbolic meaning of the statues that appear in your work. You turned to me and said: "But those are real statues. They existed in a landscape I had seen." What I think you were saying is that you always start with the fact of a living, actual setting and move from there to any universal meaning that might be contained in it.

SEFERIS

An illustration of that from someone who is a specialist in classical statues came the other day from an English scholar, who was lecturing about the statuary of the Parthenon. I went up to congratulate him after his lecture and he said to me, as I remember: "But you have a line which expresses something of what I meant when you say 'the statues are not the ruins—*we* are the ruins.' " I mean I was astonished that a scholar of his caliber was using a line from me to illustrate a point.

KEELEY

The imagery that a poet gets from his childhood is something we've discussed before. You once distinguished yourself from the average Englishman by suggesting that donkeys probably did for you what footballs and cars might do for them. I remember you also talked about the sea and the sailors of your native village near Smyrna.

SEFERIS

You know, the strange thing about imagery is that a great deal of it is subconscious and sometimes it appears in a poem and nobody knows wherefrom this emerged. But it is rooted, I am certain, in the poet's subconscious life, often of his childhood, and that's why I think it is decisive for a poet: the childhood that he has lived.

I think there are two different things functioning: conscious and subconscious memory. I think the way of poetry is to draw from the subconscious. It is not the way you write your memoirs, let's say, or the way you try to remember your past, your early life. I remember many things from my childhood which *did* impress me. For instance, when I was a child I discovered somewhere in a corner of a sort of bungalow we had in my grandmother's garden—at the place where we used to spend our summers—I discovered a compass from a ship which, as I learned afterwards, belonged to my grandfather. And that strange instrument—I think I destroyed it in the end by examining and reexamining it, taking it apart and putting it back together and then taking it apart again—became something mythical for me. Or again, when autumn approached, when there would be a rather strong wind and the fishing barges would have to sail through rough weather, we would always be glad when they were at last anchored, and my mother would say to someone among the fishermen who'd gone out: "Ah, bravo, you've come through rough weather"; and he would answer: "Madam, you know, we always sail with Charon at our side." That's moving to me. Perhaps when I wrote about Ulysses in that early poem you've commented on ["Upon a Foreign Verse"]—perhaps I had in mind some-body like that fisherman. Those "certain old sailors from my childhood" who would recite the *Erotocritos*. In any case, I think it is always a bit dangerous to make unconscious images conscious, to bring them out into the light, because, you know, they dry out immediately.

KEELEY

Have you felt any burden from having spent so many years writing for a tiny audience—an audience so small in the early years of your career that you had to publish your work at your own expense and issued something under three hundred copies of each volume. That is a situation quite unfamiliar to an established American poet.

SEFERIS

I'll give you an example. When I published my first volume, *Strophe* [Turning point], I issued 150 copies. That was in 1931. And I remember that in 1939 there were still copies available at the bookseller—copies that I withdrew from cir-culation so that I could bring out a new edition of the volume in 1940. But I must say that soon after that things began to change a bit. When I left for Egypt after the collapse of Greece in the war against Germany, I left behind me three editions of my work—*Logbook I, Mythistorima*, and *Book of Exer-cises*, besides the earlier volumes *Cistern* and *Strophe*—left them there all brand-new, without having sold a single copy before I sailed for Crete and Cairo with the Greek Govern-ment-in-exile, as you know. During my absence everything was sold out. When I came back no copies remained. The foreign occupation—enemy occupation—had given the Greek public the opportunity of concentration and reading. And I reckoned that when I returned at the end of the Occupation I was much better known in Greece than before.

KEELEY

It's a very strange phenomenon, the revival of interest in poetry during the period of the Occupation in Greece. I've heard about this from other poets: Gatsos and Elytis, for example. Poetry became an activity that brought together the Athenian intellectuals for readings and discussion, so that in a way it became the richest period for poetry in this century after the period of the thirties.

SEFERIS

Elytis published his book during the Occupation, and Gatsos his: I mean the famous *Amorgos* came out during the Occupation!

KEELEY

What happened after the Occupation? Why was there silence for so long among the leading poets?

SEFERIS

It wasn't silence. Times had changed, and horizons had widened, and everybody tried to see more of life outside the country; they were trying to find new modes of expression.

KEELEY

I wonder if you have felt anything new and interesting through reading to large public audiences in this country. The evidence of friends of mine who have no knowledge at all of Greek is that they have captured, from your reading in Greek, a different sense of the poetry's rhythm from what they get out of my reading in English.

SEFERIS

That is very important. But I can say something more about this experience of reading in America. The other day another poet reacted by sending me a poem about my reading. That is a new kind of response. But still, the important thing is to see reactions, not to be applauded or not applauded.

KEELEY

After your reading at Rutgers this fall, someone in the audience asked you what you thought of the English translations of your poetry, and you went on to make generous gestures toward your English translators, but then you added: "Of course the best translation of my poetry is in Chinese, a language which I don't understand at all."

SEFERIS

It isn't difficult to elaborate on that, because you know, I feel in languages that I know, perhaps because I know them too well (not English, but in French, for example, which I know really well) that there are other possibilities in the translation. For Chinese there are no other possibilities. But translating—I'm changing the question a little bit—is interesting always because it is a means of controlling your own language. Now, of course the English language is a more stable language than ours; we have to create ours, so to speak, all the time we are writing.

KEELEY

Pound said that translation is a means for a writer to sharpen continually his awareness of his own language, and he advised young poets to translate whenever they could.

SEFERIS

Provided you don't overdo it, I think it is always useful.

KEELEY

You are a poet who writes in a language which few people know outside Greece. I wonder if you feel any resentment of the fact that you are known in the world of poetry outside your own country largely through translation.

SEFERIS

There are compensations. For example, about a year ago, I received a letter from an American saying to me: "Well, I have learned modern Greek in order to read Seferis." That's a great compliment, I think. It is much more personal than the case of a man who learns a foreign language at school, isn't it? I've heard other people say: "Well, you know, we learned our Greek from your poems." A great reward. And then I should add, perhaps, this situation of not having a very large audience has something good in it too. I mean that it educates you in a certain way: not to consider that great audiences are the most important reward on this earth. I consider that even if I have three people who read me, I mean really read me, it is enough. That reminds me of a conversation I had once upon a time during the only glimpse I ever had of Henry Michaux. It was when he had a stopover in Athens, coming from Egypt, I think. He came ashore while his ship was in Piraeus just in order to have a look at the Acropolis. And he told me on that occasion: "You know, my dear, a man who has only one reader is not a writer. A man who has two readers is not a writer either. But a man who has *three* readers (and he pronounced "three readers" as though they were three million), that man is *really* a writer."

KEELEY

You said earlier there is a problem in Greek of establishing a language. That's something which most American readers naturally don't understand. We have a language. Our problem is always to stretch the language which we have so that it somehow shows a new vitality. When you talk about establishing or creating a language you mean something quite different.

SEFERIS

We've had the calamity of academic intervention. Mark you, I mean from both the Left and the Right. In the beginning we had the intervention of professors who wanted to transform our living language into something abstract in order to reach some sort of "idea" of a pure language. On the other side, we had the fight for *demotikí*, as we call the popular spoken language. But this tradition—the professional tradition—was so strong that there was a sort of academic mind which fought actively for both the puristic and the vernacular language. The best way to progress is by forgetting all that academic intervention. For example, I admire very much the Cretan Renaissance. In that period you find a whole poem—10,000 lines, an enormous poem—where there is no strain at all, no effort at all; the language functions quite naturally, without any flagrant tendency to be learned.

KEELEY

It's interesting that you take an effortless poem for a model, because I remember that, in another context, you described style as the difficulty one encounters in expressing oneself.

SEFERIS

I said that in lecturing about Makriyannis, who, as you know, never learned how to write or read until the age of thirty-five. When you see his manuscript, it is like a wall—a wall built up out of stones, one placed on top of the other. It is very strange. For example, he never uses punctuation at all. No paragraphs. Nothing. It goes on like that. And you see that each word is added to another word like a stone on top of another stone. I mean, in any case, that when you really feel something, you face the difficulty of expressing it. And that, after all, forms your style.

KEELEY

What are the difficulties you've encountered in establishing your own style?

SEFERIS

That's another story. In my youth I worked very much over the Greek language. Glossaries, old texts, medieval texts, and things of that kind. But the difficulty wasn't only in studying them; the difficulty was how to forget them and be natural. I had the blessing, perhaps, of being natural, I don't know. That's for others to say. . . .

KEELEY

I know you always considered it the first order of business for a poet to try for economy in style. This seems to be in contrast to the dominant mode of your predecessors—at least the mode of Palamas and Sikelianos.

SEFERIS

That's perhaps a local characteristic. I felt at the time of my early efforts that in Greece they were too rhetorical, and I reacted against it. That was my feeling. And I reacted against it in many ways. For example, in the use of words, of adjectives—especially compound adjectives, which I avoided. To avoid certain things is deliberate with me, you know. My interest in expression was not so much in the color of the language, which Greek has plenty of, but in precision above all; and in order to be precise, you have to be spare in the use of your material. You remember that Valéry said lyricism is, after all, the development of an exclamation, of an "Ah." For me "Ah" is quite enough. I never try to elaborate on the exclamation.

KEELEY

Let me pursue the matter of style as a process of using language sparingly. Do you agree that in your own work there is a development, a further economy of means, between *Strophe* and everything that followed it?

SEFERIS

Of course. It is not so much a stylistic development as a sort of evolution. Everything evolves. I mean one *has* to evolve—one *has* to see new things. One has to see other aspects and express these other aspects. Certainly there is an evolution, but I don't see it as a "development" in inverted commas. If I had years more in front of me, I would perhaps write in another way, even in another style. I might again use the strict line or rhymed verse, perhaps. In poetry you change the base of things from time to time in order to have a fresh expression.

The main thing you are looking for in poetry is to avoid worn-out expressions. That's the great problem.

KEELEY

Now what about the problem of developing a prose style. You are one of the very few poets in Greece who has had almost as strong an impact on the language of prose criticism as you've had on the language of poetry. Developing a live yet careful prose style must have been part of your struggle from the beginning.

SEFERIS

Yes, but, you know, my struggle was always for precision. That is at the base of it. And of course in prose it appears more obvious—I mean the matter of economy.

KEELEY

This tape machine seems to have stopped recording. Say something and let's see if it's still working properly.

SEFERIS

Wallace Stevens was in an insurance company.

KEELEY

Let's hope it will go on with us for a while. One of your remarks which has interested me is about the question of the relation between poetry and public service; I think you said that the important thing was for the poet not to have a job which was directly connected with that of being a poet.

SEFERIS

I didn't say the "important" thing. I don't know, really, because I can't speak for other people; but for me at least, I suppose that it is a help not to be in a job where I have to write as I write in my notebooks or poetry books. For example, I am not a professor or a teacher or even a newspaperman. I prefer to have another occupation.

KEELEY

Was there anything in your professional career—that is, the experience you had as a diplomat—which may have influenced in some way the imagery of your poetry or affected the particular themes you chose to express?

SEFERIS

I don't believe that any themes or any imagery were created by my job, though I might mention—how did you translate it?—the lines form "Last Stop": "souls shriveled up public sins, each holding office like a bird in its cage." I mean that is one of the few images I have drawn directly from my public service. But I could have felt that even if I had not been in the diplomatic service. But it was important for me that I had a job which was not related to my creative work. And the other thing is that I was not—how shall I put it?—not obliged to deal with models which belonged to literature. Of course, there are troubles in that career. The main thing I suffered from was not having enough time. Although others might tell you that it is better not to have time because it is the subconscious which is doing the poetical work. That's the point of view of Tom Eliot. I remember once, when I was transferred from London to Beirut (this was after just one and a half years of service in London), I told him: "My dear Mr. Eliot, I think I am fed up with my career and I shall give up all this." I remember his saying: "Be careful, be careful if you do that," and then he mentioned the subconscious—the subconscious working for poetry. And I told him: "Yes, but if I have a job, an official job which is interfering with my subconscious, then I prefer not to have a job. I mean I would prefer to be a carpenter and to be where my subconscious is quite free to do whatever it likes, dance or not dance." And I added: "You know, I can tell you when my public life began to interfere with my subconscious. It was on the eve of the war with the Italians—in September '40—when I started having political dreams. Then I knew quite well that my subconscious was

suffering the onslaught of my official job. 'In dreams respon-
sibilities begin.' "

KEELEY

You once made a comment about the connection between
poetry and politics . . .

SEFERIS

You mean what I've said about propaganda writing, or
"engaged" writing, or whatever you call that kind of writing
in our times. I believe that something real, as far as feeling is
concerned, should be elaborated as feeling. I don't consider
that Aeschylus was making a propaganda play by putting the
suffering Persians on stage, or desperate Xerxes, or the ghost
of Darius, and so forth. On the contrary, there was human
compassion in it. For his enemies. Not that he's not of course
glad that the Greeks won the battle of Salamis. But even then
he showed that Xerxes's defeat was a sort of divine retribu-
tion: a punishment for the hubris that Xerxes committed in
flagellating the sea. Since his hubris was to flagellate the sea,
he was punished exactly by the sea in the battle of Salamis.

KEELEY

Is it possible to compare poetry across national lines? Or
do we always have to make qualitative comparisons strictly
within a single tradition?

SEFERIS

I feel a sort of reluctance about comparing poets. It is very
difficult—even within the same tradition. Try to compare Dante
and Alfred, Lord Tennyson, for example: what that would
lead to, I don't know. Or, in the French tradition, how can
you compare Racine and Victor Hugo? You have to go very
deep, to the bottom of the tradition, in order to find some
sort of common ground where the comparison can fairly take
place. On the other hand, for example, I myself used Yeats
in my Stockholm acceptance speech because I had been read-

ing just a few months before my trip to Stockholm, "The Bounty of Sweden," where he recounts the whole affair of his election to the Nobel Prize: his trip to Stockholm, the ceremony, and everything. And there I felt a sort of relation with him as a human being—not as a poet, but as a human being; because Yeats belonged to a small country with a great folklore tradition, a country which, after all, had political turmoil. By the way, there's another example of a public poet who doesn't write propaganda. He writes, for example, a poem about an Irish airman which isn't at all propaganda. "Those I fight I do not hate—" etc. Or he writes "The Second Coming." That too is not propaganda: "The center cannot hold," etc., which after all starts somewhere in Irish political life; but it goes deeper, and that's the whole point, I think.

KEELEY

You've mentioned at your readings, in talking about "The King of Asine," the fact that it had taken you two years to find a way of writing about that particular experience, and then, at some point after having given your notes for that poem to a friend, you completed the final draft in one long evening. Eliot has implied that you finished the poem (between ten p.m. and three in the morning) exactly because you didn't have your notes before you.

SEFERIS

I had no notes. And he may have been right. I don't know. In my home in Athens, I have all my papers and my books. And I wonder if that's a helpful thing or not, if it's not better to have just a blank writing desk without any papers or any books at all, where you can sit at regular hours every day.

KEELEY

Do you normally make notes on the experience of a poem before you write it?

195

SEFERIS

Oh, there are many ways. Sometimes I do. Sometimes I do not. There are things which you have to remember, and I have to record these somewhere, so of course I make notes. For example, there is a poem where I have used the chronographer Makhairas, where it was impossible to avoid referring to that story about the demon of fornication.

KEELEY

I didn't mean notes once the poem has been composed in your mind, but notes on the experience which, in effect, becomes the poem.

SEFERIS

No, I don't do that. When I say notes, I mean there are those on the material, notes which are needed because they are descriptive. And there are notes that are ideas, poetical ideas. For example, poetical expressions, poetical utterances, that is the kind of notes I mean. If I were to write a poem about you—I might make a note that "Mike has ceased to smoke for many years." I mean if the things sound well in Greek to my ear, I could write it. That's all—things which are indifferent to other people. These I call poetical notes. Sometimes I disregard them altogether, and sometimes I go back to them. Sometimes, when they are quite forgotten, by having a glimpse at them I say: "Oh, that poem was rather interesting," although they don't say anything at all to the ordinary person. Still, they take me back to a certain atmosphere which, in the meantime, has been working, elaborating, a form in my mind.

KEELEY

Do you keep these notes or do you destroy them?

SEFERIS

Oh, I destroy a lot. Some months ago in Athens—there was somebody, a sort of Hellenist, who was interested in photographing notes. And I had the impression that I had kept my notes on *The Cistern*. I looked for them in all my files, and it appeared to me then that I had destroyed them. The only thing that I found was the "Notes for a 'Week'" which have been published quite recently—that is, the two missing poems from that group.

KEELEY

I'm sorry about that, in a way, because I think *The Cistern* is a poem that all of us have found obscure in places, and the notes might have helped—might have helped *me*, anyway.

SEFERIS

Don't complain about it. They might have made the poem much more obscure, you know. For example, the general idea about my evolution in poetry is: "Ah, you see, Seferis started with regular lines, rhymes, strict versification, and then he moved to free verse." When I see my notes, I see that the main poem of *Strophe*, the "Erotikos Logos," appears to be in very strict versification; but my notes show me that this poem was also written in free verse. I have found some of the first drafts.

KEELEY

Would you ever consider publishing them?

SEFERIS

By God, no.

KEELEY

Do you think that's the reason Eliot was so careful about not rediscovering the lost parts of *The Waste Land* which have now been rediscovered?

SEFERIS

When he told me the story about the writing of *The Waste Land*, he seemed quite desperate about the manuscripts being lost. On the other hand, he also told me how useful—he stressed that point—how *useful* the intervention of Pound had really been.

Do you approve of publishing discarded things?

I don't know, it depends. It needs a great deal of tact. Not by the poet himself, but by his editors. If they publish them they tend to stress that they are all-important discoveries, and I think this is bad. Overplaying it. The editors and the philologists are always overdoing things, I think.

I know from a section of your diary which my wife and I translated that your relationship with Eliot was an important one in your life in various ways. I wonder if any other literary figures who are known in the West have also been important to you. I'm thinking particularly of Henry Miller and Lawrence Durell and maybe others I don't know about. I'm thinking also of your own compatriots: Theotokas and Katsimbalis, for example.

Durrell was much younger than me, you know. He was a very interesting young man when I met him. He was in his mid-twenties. I met him with Henry Miller. They came to Athens to see the Colossus of Maroussi, Katsimbalis. It was on the day—if my memory is correct—of the declaration of war.

But of course Katsimbalis wasn't the Colossus at that point.

No, but Miller was threatening to make him something very colossal.

KEELEY

Well, he did.

SEFERIS

It was nice to meet them; they were, let's say the first—or if not exactly the first, then the second or third—readers with an understanding of what I was doing. For example, one of them, Miller or Larry, told me after reading my poems: "You know, what I like about you is that you turn things inside out. And I mean that in the *good* sense." That was a very nice compliment for me at that time.

KEELEY

How did they come to know your poetry?

SEFERIS

How. Hm. There were then in English only the translations of Katsimbalis. Manuscript translations, I mean.

KEELEY

When they came to Athens, why did they go directly to Katsimbalis? Why was he the man whom they approached? Was he well-known as a literary figure outside Greece?

SEFERIS

I don't know. It was a matter of common friends, perhaps. He became a bigger literary figure after *The Colossus of Maroussi*. At that time he was more in contact than I was with the English and American literary circles. There was a sort of international bohemia, I might say, by then in Athens. I mean on the eve of the war. I must add that Katsimbalis has that wonderful quality of being without evil intention in his heart. He might criticize somebody, but in a good-hearted way. And he believed that our country, our little country, was able to do something. He had that sort of belief.

KEELEY

What about Henry Miller? How did you respond to him?

SEFERIS

I like Miller because he is a very good-hearted man, and I think—excuse me for saying so, but this is not a criticism: it is great praise to say about a writer that he is a good man—Miller has a great deal of generosity in him. For example, when the moment came for him to go back to America (he was advised to do so by the American consul; as an American national, he had to go back home because the war was coming near), he said to me one day: "My dear George, you've been so kind to me, and I want to give you something." And he produced a diary which he had been keeping during his stay in Greece. I said: "Look here, Henry. But after all, I know that you are going to write a book, and you can't write the book—I mean you might need your notes." He said: "No. All those things are here," pointing to his head. I offered to make a typescript copy for him. "No," he said, "a gift must be whole." Well, that's a splendid way of behaving, I think. And I shall never forget that. The diary was a sort of first draft of the *Colossus*. But with more personal explosions. And more jokes, of course.

KEELEY

There are quite a few jokes in the book too.

SEFERIS

The trip to Hydra is splendid and the channel of Poros. Remember? My feeling about Miller is this: of course it's a great thing to have an understanding of the ancient authors; but the first man I admired for not having any classical preparation on going to Greece is Miller. There is such a freshness in him.

KEELEY

The freshness of being ready to take it all in for the first time, you mean?

SEFERIS

I suppose I was the first man to give him a text of Aeschylus, when he decided to go to Mycenae. But of course he doesn't see anything from Aeschylus; he sees, in the plain of Argos, *redskins* while he hears a jazz trumpeter. That is spontaneous behavior. And I admire it.

KEELEY

Jazz trumpeter?

SEFERIS

The jazz trumpeter was inspired, I suppose, by Louis Armstrong. Because he had heard Armstrong on a small gramophone—a quite elementary gramophone—that I had then in my home in Athens. I myself had discovered jazz eight or ten years earlier. . . .

KEELEY

Before Miller's arrival in Greece. So you taught *him* about jazz?

SEFERIS

I was thirty-two or thirty-three at that time. And I became a jazz addict. I said to myself, after all, you have discovered at the same time the importance of Bach—the great Bach— *and* the importance of jazz. I remember once I said to Mitropoulos: "For me, my dear maestro, jazz is one of the few ways left for us to express feeling without embarrassment." That was in '35. No, '34.

KEELEY

Was there any other writer abroad or in Greece with whom you had a particularly close relationship?

SEFERIS

It depends on what period you are referring to. For example, I had very close relations with Sikelianos once upon a time.

201

I met him first in 1929, though it did not become a close relationship until after his illness and my return to Greece in 1944. During his illness, Sikelianos was really remarkable, when he had all those crises in his health. While I was serving abroad I would take advantage of my trips to Athens to go and see him. One time I heard that he had just been through a sort of cerebral hemorrhage. I found him at the theater wearing dark glasses—a première at the National Theater. I said: "Oh Angelo, I am so glad you are here, because I had heard that you were not so well." "My dear," he said, "it is such a splendid thing to have a little ruby on the top of your brain." He meant the hemorrhage. I said to him: "It is a splendid thing that you can talk about it that way. I am so glad." He said: "George, look here. I shall tell you a story during the next intermission." I approached him during the next intermission. He said: "Have you read *Rocambol*?" It's a sort of French thriller. Sikelianos went on: "Once upon a time a woman had thrown vitriol against the face of Rocambol, and Rocambol was in danger of losing his eyesight; so he was taken by one of his henchmen to the best specialist in Paris, and the specialist examined him very carefully while the friend of Rocambol was sitting in the waiting room overhearing the conversation of the doctor. And the doctor's conclusion was: "Sir, you have to choose between two things: either lose your eyesight or be disfigured." There was a moment of heavy silence, then the voice from the waiting room, the voice of the friend of Rocambol was heard: "Rocambol has no need of his eyesight."

KEELEY

Tell me more about Sikelianos. So little is known about him outside Greece.

SEFERIS

Another thing which I have mentioned in writing, at the time of his death. He had a great crisis in Athens and I rushed to see him; I was very anxious; he had collapsed in the house of a friend. And again, the same splendid reaction. I said to him: "My dear Angelo, are you all right?" He said: "I'm all right. But I had a splendid experience. I saw the absolute dark. It was so beautiful."

KEELEY

Did you know Palamas? What kind of man was he?

SEFERIS

You know, it is strange the memories I have kept of people. For example, other people admire Sikelianos for their own special reasons; myself, I was attracted by those tragic and splendid moments of Sikelianos's last years. Now Palamas: one of my last memories of him was when I went to tell him good-bye because I was leaving shortly. During our conversation, he referred to various crazy people mentioned in his poetry and added: "You know, we have many mad people in my family. I wanted once upon a time to write a book called 'To Genos ton Loxon.'" How can we translate that into English? "The breed of . . ."

KEELEY

Of madmen.

SEFERIS

Not quite of madmen. Of "oblique" men.

KEELEY

Oblique men?

SEFERIS

I'm trying to get the precise translation of the word.

KEELEY

Unbalanced men, perhaps.

SEFERIS

I said to him: "Mr. Palamas, it is a pity you *didn't* write such a book." Because I thought it would be a good book. He had an interesting sense of humor.

KEELEY

What do you consider Palamas's most significant contribution to Greek literature?

SEFERIS

Well, I said it in *Dokimes*, but I would repeat: his very important contribution to the Greek language. I mean compared to his, Cavafy's expression seems rather faint, although at certain moments more real.

KEELEY

But the minute you say "although more real" . . .

SEFERIS

Again, what I appreciate very much in Cavafy is his having started with terrifically unreal poems and then, by insistence and work, he found at last his own personal voice. He wrote very bad poems up to his thirty-fourth year. The failure of those poems cannot be translated or communicated to a foreign reader because the language of the translation is always bound to improve them. There is no possibility of translating that sort of thing faithfully.

You know, what I admire—let me put it my own way— what I admire about Cavafy was this: he was a man who starts at a certain age with all signs showing that he's unable to produce anything of importance. And then, by refusing and refusing things which are offered him, in the end he *finds*, he *sees*, as they say; he becomes certain that he's found his own expression. It's a splendid example of a man who, through his refusals, finds his way.

KEELEY

What did he refuse precisely?

SEFERIS

Expressions, and the easy things, verbosity—that sort of thing. Take his poem on ancient tragedy, for example. It is very bad. It is something unbelievable. By putting aside things like that, Cavafy improves his expression up to the end of his life, even up to the last poem he wrote on the outskirts of Antioch: the happenings between the Christians and Julian. And I admire him for going on to the end like that. He's a great example. He had the courage, up to the end of his life, not to admit certain things, to reject them. And that's why I have doubts about all these people who are trying to put into circulation all the rejected writings of Cavafy, unless one is very careful in reading him. You know, that needs a great deal of discernment.

KEELEY

To turn now to the other well-known writer of the older generation, what about Kazantzakis? In the U.S., Cavafy is the poet who's respected by those who are themselves poets—Auden, for instance, and many of the important younger American poets; most of them know Cavafy and most of them have a sympathetic attitude toward him. But among students and among those who are just beginning to learn about literature, Kazantzakis is by far the most popular Greek writer, both as poet and as novelist. Increasingly my job is to try to discuss Kazantzakis's work—whether poetry or fiction—without diminishing him.

SEFERIS

I don't wonder. The thing is that one must have a possibility of being in contact with a writer, and that I cannot do in the case of Kazantzakis—a terrible thing for me, you know. I must give you a warning as far as Kazantzakis is concerned. On the one hand, there is his poetry—what is called poetry—

and that's the *Odyssey* sequel, of course, and his plays in verse; and on the other hand, there is his prose: the novels. Now, as far as the novels are concerned, I am not competent to judge. I don't know how to speak about the novels. I have not read all of them. I hear from poeple whom I trust that they are very good, and they may well *be* very good. But the *Odyssey* sequel is another matter. There, although you have interesting passages, I'm afraid there is no poetry in them. I say interesting passages—passages that are informative about the man Kazantzakis; but I don't believe that's poetry, at least not the poetry I believe in.

KEELEY

What about as "idea," quite aside from poetic considerations? As statement of a philosophical or religious position.

SEFERIS

I don't know. I have no idea about philosophical positions and world-views. You know, whenever world-views begin interfering with writing—I don't know. I prefer world-views in the sort of dry, repulsive, and (I don't know how to put it) prosaic way. I don't like people who try to express world-views in writing poetry. I remember once I had a reading in Thessaloniki, and a philosopher stood up and asked: "But what, after all, Mr. Seferis, is your world-view?" And I said: "My dear friend, I'm sorry to say that I have no world-view. I have to make this public confession to you that I am writing without having any world-view. I don't know, perhaps you find that scandalous, sir, but may I ask you to tell me what Homer's world-view is?" And I didn't get an answer.

KEELEY

To move on to a more general subject, you said during one of our conversations in Athens that a circumstance which is notable about Greek writers in this century was that so many of them were outside the Kingdom of Greece proper. You mentioned yourself as an instance, having been brought up in Smyrna. Could you comment on the ways your Smyrna origin may have influenced your work or your general role as a man of letters?

SEFERIS

Let me say that I am interested in everything which finds expression in the Greek language and in Greek lands—I mean taking Greek lands as a whole. For example, I was terribly interested, as you know, in what happened in Crete in the 17th century. And in another way, people in Roumania, for example, the principalities of Moldavia and Wallachia, interested me very much—even odd minor people like Kaisarios Dapontes, if you know who he is. I think he was from somewhere in the northern islands, Skopelos of the Sporades, and he lived a long part of his life in the principalities, then Constantinople, and finally he retired to Mt. Athos under the name of Kaisarios. I don't mean that he is a great poet, simply that his way of expressing himself interests me. I don't say that he writes great poetry, but after all, one feels that in those countries in the 18th century, there was such a flourishing of Greek letters. Another monk of Mt. Athos—I'm trying to remember his name—yes, his name was Pamberis, wrote a poem, not a very long one because it would be an impossible achievement to write a long poem under the system he decided to use. He called it "Poiema Karkinikon," so to say, "Poem Cancerous." It was devised so that it could be read from left to right or from right to left, and still attempting to make sense—but a sense so remote that he had to put notes explaining what each line meant. These small details amuse me, you know. And I think that they add to the too-professional image we have of Greek literature. Or again, another text: "The Mass of the Beardless Man." It is a text written in the form of a mock Mass that parodies the Mass in a rather shocking way. It amuses me especially because I don't see enough light comic texts in our literature. Either people refrained from writing such texts, or such texts were eliminated by somber-minded academics.

KEELEY

That's an interesting remark. You've said on another occasion that one thing which you find that the Anglo-Saxon tradition has and no other tradition has is that element of nonsense—an element which is fairly continuous in our literature and which seems always to have existed in some form.

SEFERIS

The Anglo-Saxon tradition is certainly different from ours in that respect; and I believe that no continental country can claim the same kind of nonsense that Edward Lear and Lewis Carroll offer.

KEELEY

You've spent three periods of service in England, spread over the best part of your literary career. Did you find it an especially congenial climate for work?

SEFERIS

Not really. A very good place for me for writing was when I was in Albania, because I was quite unknown there, and very isolated; at the same time I was near Greece, I mean from the language point of view, and I could use my free time to advantage. There were no exhausting social functions.

KEELEY

What about your acquaintance with English men of letters during your early years in England? You met Eliot, of course.

SEFERIS

No, I had a letter of introduction to Eliot and I rang his office, but the secretary informed me that Eliot was in the United States. It was the time when he was Charles Eliot Norton Professor at Harvard. I never met Eliot nor any other writer in the beginning. First of all, I was rather shy as a person; then, it was a period when I was groping to find my own further expression. In contrast, when I came to England after World War II, my period in the Middle East had created a great many friends among the English, and when I came back to England as Counselor at the Embassy, I had no difficulty at all, because by then I was quite well known in England. It was just after the publication of my first translation into English, *The King of Asine and Other Poems*, in 1948.

KEELEY

During the period of your first official visit to England, I wonder whether you had any contact with English or American literature that you found particularly exciting along with Eliot's work.

SEFERIS

I think a very instructive man for me, as I found out afterwards, was W. B. Yeats. But I'm talking about Yeats's early period. After all, you see, I had endeavored to exploit folklore much as Yeats did.

KEELEY

What about American literature? Did you have any favorite American authors in your formative years?

SEFERIS

It is an odd thing for us—I suppose that happens to everybody abroad—I mean one gets into literature and art by chance. For example, I don't remember on what occasion I came to know Archibald MacLeish. And I translated him, as a matter of fact. I think I am the first man to have translated him in Greece. Then there was Marianne Moore. I had translated Marianne Moore before the war also. "The Monkeys," "To a Snail."

KEELEY

You say you encountered them by accident. What was the accident?

SEFERIS

Oh, I don't know. Some review where I saw the poems, I don't remember which one. And again, Ezra Pound. I had already translated three *Cantos* before the war.

KEELEY

When I brought up American literature, I was really thinking about the older American poets: Walt Whitman and Emily Dickinson, for example.

SEFERIS

I knew Walt Whitman. Because I started with French literature, and Walt Whitman was translated into French early enough to be available to me. And then Henry Miller had an admiration for Whitman. He gave me many hints about him. That was quite near the outbreak of the war, of course. But I keep reading Whitman, as, in my youth, I was reading Edgar Allan Poe.

KEELEY

Now that you're about to go back to Greece, do you have anything that you can say about this particular visit to the United States—which is your third visit, if I'm not mistaken—anything about your impressions of this country.

SEFERIS

My third visit to America has been the most important of all, this visit; it has been more substantial than the others. I don't believe that visiting New York helps you to understand America. Curiously enough, I am now in the middle of a wood in a remote place, Princeton, yet I have been able to see and understand more of America from this remote place than if I were in a great center.

KEELEY

Of course Princetonians don't think Princeton is all that remote.

SEFERIS

Well, I mean for others who are trying, when they are traveling, to see cosmopolitan centers, it might look remote. And after all, we travelers do not attend courses at the university.

KEELEY

What have you seen in particular during this visit that has impressed you?

SEFERIS

I don't want to mention things which impress me, you know. Nobody knows what impresses him on the spot. I mean it takes time to be elaborated somehow by memory.

KEELEY

Did you get some work done?

SEFERIS

Yes, I think I did. I can't say. I don't know how to speak about work done. I have the impression that one can speak about work done only when the work is finished. I am not inclined to speak about my work during the period of elaboration. But in any case, there is an inner feeling that you have not lost your time. Which is something. I mean I want to be honest with you: I cannot mention anything really done. The only thing I can mention to you—and I'm not going to mention the substance of it—is that I wrote a poem of two lines.

KEELEY

You just received a volume of Eugene McCarthy's poems. I found that rather moving: to discover that he had in fact written a volume of poems, and apparently during his campaign last year.

Yes, why not? I mean I can very well understand that. If there was a period of euphoria, there is no reason why it shouldn't happen in poetry at the same time that it happens in a chapter of politics. One of my poems, "*Thrush*," was written after a terribly active period of my life—I mean politically active, because I was principal private secretary to the Regent of Greece, just before going to Poros. Of course, poems do not appear like an eruption by a volcano; they need preparation. And as I think back on "*Thrush*," I can well mark notes, lines, which I had started writing during the previous year, that most active year. Nevertheless, I remember days when the job was killing, because I was not a politician, I was just a servant, a public servant, and I remember days when I started going to my office at something like eight o'clock in the morning and returned back home the next day at five o'clock in the morning, without having had any meal or any sleep. I mention that, of course, not in order to move you but in order to show you that, after all, time was pressing then. But I was also writing. Of course, there are other things which influenced my work at that time, and among other things, I might mention the fact that I returned to my country after a great period of longing, at the end of the war.

Do you feel that, in addition to the lines you wrote, the poem was gestating in some significant way during this very active period, so that when you went to Poros it could come out as the coherent work it is in a relatively short period? A month of vacation, wasn't it?

Two months. The first long holiday I ever had during my career—the longest one.

And you were able to write the poem—and it is a long

poem—in effect during one sitting: the long sitting of that two-month vacation?

SEFERIS

No. You'll find the story of my writing that poem in the diary of this period, the period of '46 on Poros. I used to go for a swim—no, first I would cut wood in the garden (which was a huge garden), then go to the sea, and then work up to night, up to darkness, which started at seven o'clock. And it is strange, you know, how—excuse me for talking like this— I noticed how one is cleansed progressively by such a life. For example, I noticed that cleansing in my dreams, as I mentioned in this diary which has been recently published.

KEELEY

I have only one more really general topic to bring up. I wonder if you feel, as the result of your rather unique position in Greek letters now—I suppose any poet has a unique position in his country once he's won the Nobel Prize—if you feel that this in any way has affected your sense of a public role as a man of letters as distinct from your private role as a poet—any responsibility you may feel toward younger poets, for instance, toward the cultural life around you, or any position you may sense you have to maintain in relation to your country.

SEFERIS

I should from the beginning tell you quite bluntly—if I can say it in English—that the Nobel Prize is an accident, no more than an accident. It's not an appointment. And I have no feeling that I have been appointed to any sort of function. It is just an accident which one has to try and forget as soon as possible. Otherwise, if you are overdazzled by that sort of thing, you get lost and founder. At the time I won the prize, there was a sort of—how can I put it in English?—a sort of Cassandra-like critic who wrote that Seferis should be very careful because he's going to be completely dried up as far as his work is concerned and even die from various illnesses since that sort of thing happens to people who have that kind of success. He was just exaggerating the one side of it, without considering, after all, what showed in the way I reacted to the prize. For example, I said in Stockholm to my judges (or whatever they are): "Gentlemen, I thank you"—this at the end of a sort of lecture I gave there—"for allowing me, after a long effort, to be *nobody*, to be unnoticed, as Homer says of Ulysses." And I was quite sincere. After all, I don't recognize the right of anybody to take you by the back of your neck and throw you into a sort of ocean of empty responsibilities. Why, that's scandalous after all.

KEELEY

Now let's move away from the issue of the Nobel Prize. Greece, being a small country, seems to me to have always had, somehow, a tradition (it's an informal tradition, unlike the British one) of an unofficial but generally recognized poet laureate—a feeling among poets and their followers that there is one spokesman for poetry in each particular generation—even if the role of spokesman is sometimes self-assumed. Sikelianos, for example, played that role. And in his day, so did Palamas.

SEFERIS

Well, yes, God bless them, but I'm sorry to say that I never felt I was the spokesman for anything or anybody. There are no credentials which appoint anybody to be spokesman for something. Now others consider that a sort of function which must be performed; but I think that is, after all, why I have written so little. I've never felt the obligation; I have to consider only that I am not dried up as a poet and to write. I mean that has been my feeling from the very beginning. I remember when I published my first book, there were lots of people who said: "Mr. Seferis, you must now try to show us that you can do more." I answered them: "Gentlemen, you must consider that every poem published by me is the last one. I never have any feeling about its continuation." My last poem. And if I write another one, it's a great blessing. Now how much I have worked in order to produce the next poem, or how much I have not worked, is another matter—a private matter. Others think that they are the voices of the country. All right. God bless them. And sometimes they've been very good in that function.

KEELEY

Joyce felt that way a bit. I'm thinking of the famous remark by Stephen Dedalus at the end of *A Portrait of the Artist as a Young Man*, "to forge in the smithy of my soul the uncreated conscience of my race."

SEFERIS

I can give you another example. In my youth there was an enormous amount of discussion about the problem of knowing, or trying to define, what is Greek and what is not Greek—praising one thing as Greek and condemning something else as un-Greek: trying, in short, to establish "the real" Greek tradition. So I wrote, "Greekness is the sum of the authentic works which are going to be produced by Greeks." We cannot say that we have *some* works creating the conscience of Greece. We see a line, but surrounded by large margins of darkness. It isn't simple. I don't know what my voice is. If others, for the time being, consider that it is *their* conscience, so much the better. It's up to them to decide. It's not up to me to impose; because you cannot be a sort of dictator in these matters.

KEELEY

Some would think yours the healthy attitude, but there are other people who feel that a Nobel Prize winner, especially when he is the only one the country has ever had, *ought* to be a spokesman and a public conscience.

SEFERIS

It might be so, but, after all, one takes the attitude which is imposed on him by his nature, or whatever you call it. At the same time, I have never forced myself to write anything which I didn't think necessary. When I say "necessary," I mean which I *had* to express or be smothered.

KEELEY

Well, I've run out of questions. Since you don't have any grand advice for the younger generation, I've nothing more to ask you.

SEFERIS

I *have* advice.

KEELEY

Oh, you *do*? Good.

SEFERIS

I have the following advice to give to the younger Greek generation: to try to exercise themselves as much as they can in the modern Greek language. And not to write it upside down. I have to tell them that in order to write, one must believe in what one does, not seeming to believe that one is believing something. They must remember that the only job in which one cannot lie is poetry. You can't lie in poetry. If you are a liar, you'll always be discovered. Perhaps now, perhaps in five years, in ten years, but you are going to be discovered eventually if you are lying.

KEELEY

When you speak of lying, you're speaking first of all about lying about your emotional . . .

SEFERIS

I don't know what I mean. Perhaps it is an emotional thing. In the reality of one's thoughts. I don't know. I mean there is a special sound about the solid, the sound thing. You knock against it, and it renders a sort of sound which proves that it is genuine.

KEELEY

Do you think every writer always knows himself whether the sound he hears is genuine or not?

SEFERIS

No. It is difficult to say. But he must somehow have an instinct—a guiding instinct—which says to him: "My dear boy, my dear chap, be careful; you are going to fall. You are exaggerating at this moment." And then, when he hears that, he should not take a drug in order to say to himself: "Why, you are all right, my dear." You are not all right, my dear, at all.

BIBLIOGRAPHICAL NOTE

I. Short titles (arranged alphabetically)

Analogies of Light
Odysseus Elytis: Analogies of Light, ed. Ivar Ivask (Norman, Okla., 1981).
The Axion Esti
Odysseus Elytis: The Axion Esti, trans. Edmund Keeley and George Savidis (Pittsburgh, 1974; London, 1980).
Cavafy: Collected Poems
C. P. Cavafy: Collected Poems, trans. Edmund Keeley and Philip Sherrard, ed. George Savidis (Princeton and London, 1975).
Cavafy's Alexandria
Edmund Keeley, *Cavafy's Alexandria: Study of a Myth in Progress* (Cambridge and London, 1976).
Encyclopedia of Poetry and Poetics
Encyclopedia of Poetry and Poetics, ed. Alex Preminger (Princeton, 1965, 1974).
"The Language of Irony"
Nasos Vayenas, "The Language of Irony (Towards a Definition of the Poetry of Cavafy)," *Byzantine and Modern Greek Studies*, Vol. 5 (1979).
"A Letter on '*Thrush*' "
"George Seferis, "A Letter on '*Thrush*,' " *Anglohellenic Review*, Vol. 4, No. 12 (July-August, 1950). English translation by James Stone in *Journal of the Hellenic Diaspora*, Vol. 7, No. 2 (Summer, 1980).

The Lost Center
 Zissimos Lorenzatos, *The Lost Center and Other Essays in Greek Poetry*, trans. Kay Cicellis (Princeton, 1980).
On the Greek Style
 George Seferis, *On the Greek Style: Selected Essays in Poetry and Hellenism*, trans. Rex Warner and Th. D. Frangopoulos (New York and London, 1966).
Ritsos in Parentheses
 Edmund Keeley, *Ritsos in Parentheses* (Princeton, 1979).
Seferis: Collected Poems
 George Seferis: Collected Poems, trans. Edmund Keeley and Philip Sherrard (Princeton and London, 1981).
Sikelianos: Selected Poems
 Angelos Sikelianos: Selected Poems, trans. Edmund Keeley and Philip Sherrard (Princeton and London, 1979).
Six Poets of Modern Greece
 Six Poets of Modern Greece, trans. Edmund Keeley and Philip Sherrard (London, 1960; New York, 1961).
Vayenas: *The Poet and the Dancer*
 Nasos Vayenas, *The Poet and the Dancer: An Examination of the Poetics and the Poetry of Seferis* (Athens, 1979).

II. First serial publication of the essays included in this volume

 "Cavafy's Voice and Context," *"Grand Street* (Spring, 1983).
 "Angelos Sikelianos: The Sublime Voice," *The Ontario Review*, No. 11 (Fall-Winter, 1979-1980).
 "Ancient Greek Myth in Angelos Sikelianos," *Byzantine and Modern Greek Studies*, Vol. 7 (1981).
 "Seferis's Elpenor: A Man of No Fortune," *The Kenyon Review*, Vol. 28, No. 3 (June, 1966).

"Seferis and the 'Mythical Method,' " *Comparative Literature Studies*, Vol. 6, No. 2 (June, 1969).

"George Seferis," *Encounter*, Vol. 38, No. 3 (March, 1972).

"The Voices of Elytis' *The Axion Esti*," *Books Abroad*, Vol. 49, No. 4 (Autumn, 1975).

"Elytis and the Greek Tradition," *The Charioteer* (forthcoming).

"Yannis Ritsos in Parentheses," *Boston University Journal*, Vol. 25, No. 3 (1978).

"The Art of Poetry XIII: George Seferis," *The Paris Review*, No. 50 (Fall, 1970). It also appeared in *Writers at Work: The Paris Review Interviews*, edited by George Plimpton. Copyright © by The Paris Review, Inc. Reprinted by permission of Viking Penguin Inc.

SUBJECT INDEX

absence, theme in Ritsos, 159, 167
Achmatova, Anna, 164
Adonis, 79, 147
Aegean, the, 54; in Elytis, 132, 137
Aeschylus, 32, 104, 118, 194, 201; *Agamemnon*, 105, 111; *The Persians*, 100, 101; in Seferis, 105
Ai Strati, Ritsos's incarceration on, 150n
Ajax, in Seferis, 98
Alcmene, 38
Alexander of Selefkia, 26, 26n
Alexander the Great, 28, 130; in Seferis, 60
Alexandria, 26, 26n, 29
alienation: theme in Ritsos, 167, 168, 175; in Sikelianos, 36
anachronism: in Seferis, 55, 61; in Seferis's "Mythistorima," 80
ancient gods: in Elytis, 127; in Ritsos, 159, 160; in Seferis, 53; in Sikelianos, 33, 48, 143
ancient Greece: characters from, in Ritsos, xvi; Seferis's view of, 55, 145, 183; sources from, xv, 51; survival of, 143. *See also* past and present
Andromache, 103
Antioch, 24, 26, 26n
Apollo, 98
apostrophe, in Cavafy, 17, 20
Ardiaios, 112
Argonauts, in Seferis, 60, 93

Argos, 103
Aristotle, 130
Armstrong, Louis, 201
Asia Minor, 27
Asine, 82
attitude: poet's, 6; in Cavafy, 13, 19, 23, 27n; speaker's, 6; in Cavafy, 13, 19, 26n
Auden, W. H., 4, 15, 16, 30, 49n, 50, 205; "Musée des Beaux Arts," 49

Babylas, *see* Varylas
Bach, 201
Beaton, Roderick, 3, 15, 30
Beirut, 24, 26n; in Cavafy, 26
Beresford, Commander Lord Hugh, 100
Bien, Peter, xiin
biography, in Cavafy, 30
Breton, André, 135, 144
Breughel's *Icarus*, 50
Brodsky, Joseph, 12
Byzantine tradition, xvi, 130; in Elytis, 136, 138, 139

Carlyle, Thomas, 65
Carroll, Lewis, 208
catharsis: in Ritsos, 178; in Sikelianos, 36
Cavafy, C. P., 31, 32, 45, 61, 62, 68, 74, 89n, 99, 120, 131, 204; ancient Alexandrians in, 12; "autonomous dramatic world" in,

Index of Works

230

OTHER BOOKS BY EDMUND KEELEY

FICTION
The Libation
The Gold-Hatted Lover
The Impostor
Voyage to a Dark Island

POETRY IN TRANSLATION
Six Poets of Modern Greece (with Philip Sherrard)
George Seferis: Collected Poems, 1924-1955 (with Philip Sherrard)
C. P. Cavafy: Passions and Ancient Days (with George Savidis)
C. P. Cavafy: Selected Poems (with Philip Sherrard)
Odysseus Elytis: The Axion Esti (with George Savidis)
C. P. Cavafy: Collected Poems (with Philip Sherrard and George Savidis)
Angelos Sikelianos: Selected Poems (with Philip Sherrard)
Ritsos in Parentheses
The Dark Crystal/Voices of Modern Greece (with Philip Sherrard)
Odysseus Elytis: Selected Poems (ed. with Philip Sherrard)
George Seferis: Collected Poems (with Philip Sherrard)
Yannis Ritsos: Return and Other Poems, 1967-1972

FICTION IN TRANSLATION
Vassilis Vassilikos: The Plant, The Well, The Angel (with Mary Keeley)

CRITICISM
Modern Greek Writers (ed. with Peter Bien)
Cavafy's Alexandria: Study of a Myth in Progress

LIBRARY OF CONGRESS
CATALOGING IN PUBLICATION DATA

Keeley, Edmund.
Modern Greek poetry.

Bibliography: p.   Includes index.
1. Greek poetry, Modern—20th century—History and
criticism—Addresses, essays, lectures.   I. Title.
PA5250.K44   1984   889'.13'09   83-11041
ISBN 0-691-06586-1